HEROINES
Women in the Bible Who Changed the World

ASHER INTRATER
with foreword and afterword by Jane Hansen Hoyt

Heroines: Women in the Bible Who Changed the World

Published By:
Revive Israel Media
206 East 4th Street
Frederick, MD 21701
www.reviveisrael.org

Cover design and interior layout by www.PearCreative.ca

ISBN 978-1-941941-90-4
Copyright © 2015 by Asher Intrater
Printed in the United States of America

All translations in this book are the author's. Translations from the Hebrew Scriptures are direct from the original Hebrew. Translations of the New Covenant are a reconstruction adapted from the Modern Hebrew Translation (The Bible Society in Israel). Hebrew text translations are occasionally compared to the New King James Version, © Thomas Nelson Publishers.

TABLE OF CONTENTS

INTRODUCTION

Some of the greatest heroes of the Bible are not heroes at all but heroines. This book is a study of a dozen of those key women who paved the way for all of us who walk by faith in the God of Israel.

In studying these women of faith, we will find a deep mystery of Scriptures, an insight into the secret plan of God, which He designed before the foundation of the earth. By understanding faith from the point of view of these women, this mysterious revelation can be found.

We are delighted to have not only a foreword to the book by Jane Hansen Hoyt of Aglow International but also a brilliant special supplement written by her describing how the unity of men and women reflects the entire plan of God to unite all things through Messiah Yeshua.

This book is designed to be a devotional study. It deals with issues of the heart. In my own personal prayers, I feel identification with these 12 special women. I try to "put myself in their shoes" and receive the inspiration and insights that they had.

This is not a book about women; it is a book about prayer and devotion. The women described here serve as models of faith and love, and we can all follow and identify with them, whether we are men or women.

I want to share that identification with you in the hope that it will bring you encouragement and inspiration, as well as increase the effectiveness and intimacy of your prayers on a daily basis.

In Yeshua's Love,
Asher

FOREWORD
By Jane Hansen Hoyt

Looking back in history, we can see that God has always used women. Many times God's ongoing plan seemed to hinge on the response of a woman. As we read through Scripture, it appears that when God worked through women, He worked primarily through individual women – Jochabed, Sarah, Deborah, Abagail, Esther, and many others whom you will read about in this book.

Consider Jochabed for example. During perilous times for the nation of Israel, God looked for someone He could use to set in motion His plan for the deliverance of His people (Ex. 1-2). He found Jochabed: a woman of faith, a woman of courage, a woman who would be willing to stand in the face of the enemy to see God's will fulfilled in the earth. It would be easy to miss the influence of Jochabed's part in the larger plan because she would do what seemed natural for a woman. She would respond out of the very essence of her womanhood, out of her "mother's heart" to protect her newborn son, Moses. You know the rest of the story.

God's ongoing plan for His people seemed to hinge on the response of a woman.

Consider Sarah. God had given a promise to Abraham and Sarah (Gen 17). From them would come a great nation and ultimately, the Promised Seed of Genesis 3:15. But there was a problem: Sarah was barren. Unless God first dealt with the barrenness in Sarah, the prophetic word over their lives would be just that: a word. We know that in her humanness, Sarah tried to "help" God by giving her maidservant, Hagar, to her husband. That's not the kind of "help" God had in mind when He created Eve! Yet God healed Sarah and she did, indeed, bring forth the promised son and through him, the continuation of God's ongoing plan in the earth. We're told in Hebrews 11:11, "Sarah received strength to conceive," and responded to God.

God's ongoing plan for His people seemed to hinge on the response of a woman.

Consider Abigail. Her husband, Nabal, had offended the then-future-king of Israel, David, by not only denying David's request, but scornfully insulting David's character and value. Acting out of concern for her household that was about to be destroyed by David's men, Abigail fashions a plan birthed out of the wisdom and understanding that was in her heart. When she meets David, she not only apologizes for the behavior of her husband, she speaks prophetically into David's destiny as the future king, thereby protecting him from "needless bloodshed or vengeance" (1 Sam 25:30-31). You how this story ends: David's anger is allayed and Abigail ultimately becomes queen.

God's ongoing plan for His people seemed to hinge on the response of a woman.

Countless other women in the Bible, and in our lifetimes, have been used by God to further His plan and purpose in the earth. As I mentioned, it has been primarily been through the actions of individual women who, out of the essence of their womanhood, cooperated with God in furthering His plan in the earth.

However, never in all of history has there been the kind of corporate calling forth or worldwide awakening among women such as we have seen in the past 48 years. Aglow International was birthed during this time in response to the massive heart cry of women to know more of God. My association with Aglow since the earliest days of the ministry has given me an experiential view of what God has been doing in the hearts of women on many fronts around the world.

Why is this awakening so critical and how does it figure into God's overall plan and purpose for mankind? I believe it is because women have a crucial role in God's end-time plan. He has been healing, restoring and bringing women into an understanding of their God-given identity and destiny so that His purpose for the body of Messiah can be realized.

God is about a final, critical restoration of what was begun in the Garden of Eden at the dawn of creation. When God created male and female and told them to multiply and take dominion in the earth, He set in place the foundation of His plan. It was the structure He chose to express His image in the earth and that structure was male and female. This was God's Plan A. There was no Plan B. This was to be a microcosm of the Church: male and female. The destiny of the body of Messiah began here.

In order for the church to display the strength, anointing and impact God intended, the relationship between male and female must be restored. While we see this in the context of marriage, it goes beyond the marriage union and encompasses the relationship between men and women in the body of Christ. The dominion God intended in the beginning will never come through men alone walking in authority. It must come with women moving into their place of God-given authority, strength and dignity in the earth.

As you read the stories of the heroines in the pages of this book, keep in mind the larger impact of their lives in God's purposes in the earth. Understand the influence each one had when, responding out of the core of her femaleness, she became part of God's unfolding end-time scenario. Purpose to glean the principles they illustrate for your own life, whether you are a man or a woman. And finally, ask the Holy Spirit to reveal to you how you may apply those principles to your circumstances.

1

Queen Esther

THE GLORIFIED BRIDE

(BOOK OF ESTHER)

The creation of Adam and Eve, or man and woman, was part of the pre-destined, secret plan of God. God created Adam and Eve with a purpose. That purpose was to reflect His glory.

The Hebrew for "man" or "Adam" is the same word: adam. **Genesis 1:26 – "Let us make adam in our image, according to our likeness: let them have dominion …"** God created Adam (man) in His image.

But then the next verse says that God created man in His image as "male and female." **Genesis 1:27 – So God created adam in His own image; in the image of God He created him; male**

and female He created them. Adam or Man was both the male and the female together. Together they were the image of God.

In Genesis chapter 2 the Bible gives more detail saying that Adam was created first in the image of God, but then God said it was not good for him to be alone (**Genesis 2:18**). Therefore He created the woman to be the helpmate and companion for the man (**Genesis 2:18, 23**). More than just a helpmate, she was to be the object of his love and to become one with him (**Genesis 2:24**).

The creation of Adam and Eve has a profound meaning in the plan of God. Adam is the image of God and therefore also the image of the Messiah to come. The Christ-Messiah is the ultimate image of God in the form of man and man in the form of God. Yeshua is the fulfillment of the original purpose of Adam (**I Corinthians 15:45**).

Who is to be the companion of the God-Man-Christ-Messiah? The woman figure is the bride. The "Bride" is that group of people who have made covenant with God from every nation of the world, which starts and ends with the nation of Israel. Ultimately, the Church and Israel are one. The people of God are to be one.

The companion/helpmate/co-ruler of the Messiah is Israel, the Church, the Ecclesia, the Kehilah, the people of God. The Church is the Bride of Christ. This is a profound secret of the Kingdom of God. **Ephesians 5:32 – This is a great mystery; I am referring to Christ and the Church.** (In fact, the image of man and woman is a foundational pattern for other mysteries in the Bible, including the unity between Israel and the Church – **Ephesians 2:15-16**, and the restoration of heaven and earth – **Ephesians 1:10; Revelation 21:2, 10.**)

As it was not good for Adam to be without Eve, so it is not good for Christ to be without the Church. The two go together like love and marriage. Adam was the seed image of Yeshua the Messiah. Eve was the seed image of the Church/Ecclesia as the Bride of Christ. Yeshua is the Prince, the King. The Church is the Princess, the Queen, standing at His side.

Psalm 45:9-14
Kings' daughters are among Your honorable women; at Your right hand stands the queen in gold from Ophir...The King will greatly desire your beauty; because He is your Lord, worship Him...The royal daughter is all glorious within the palace; her clothing is woven with gold. She shall be brought to the King in robes of many colors.

Ultimately, the glory of God will dwell in both Christ and the Church, or as we Messianics say, in Messiah and the Kehilah. **Ephesians 3:21 – Glory to God in the Church and in Christ Jesus.** The two together reflect the full, double glory of God. Just as God will be glorified through Yeshua, so will He be glorified in the Ecclesia—the Church—the group of people throughout the world who believe in Him.

The image of the Church is a glorified bride, ruling and reigning next to her husband, the King Messiah. Thus, God receives a double glory, a parallel glory, through both Yeshua and the People of God, His Bride. The Queen is glorified, standing next to the King.

Before Adam and Eve sinned, they did not notice they were naked (**Genesis 2:25**). It is possible that the reason they did not notice was that they were filled with the glory of God. When they sinned, the glory left and they noticed their embarrassing nakedness. The point is that before they sinned, Adam and Eve were closer to being the image of Christ and the Church (Messiah and the Kehilah) than most husbands and wives are today.

In the future the international Ecclesia will achieve her full glory as the partner bride of Yeshua. She will be fully glorified and stand with Him (**Revelation 12:1; Psalm 45:9, 13**). If I could pick any human being in history who came closest to the image of Yeshua ruling on earth and reigning in glory as a king over his Kingdom, I would have to say Solomon (**Matthew 12:42**). [Of course I am referring to Solomon at the height of his reign, before he sinned.]

If you could pick any woman in history who came closest to the image of the Church as the glorified bride of Christ, who would you pick? My choice would be Queen Esther. She is the ultimate princess, the ultimate daughter of Zion, both a queen and a beauty queen.

Esther is an amazing image of God's glorious plan for the human race ruling and reigning with King Messiah on the earth. She has such a significant role in the plan of God and ranks among the great heroes of the faith. More than any other person, she fulfilled the image of the glorified bride.

She was not only a bride, but she was a beauty queen. She is the biblical "Miss World" - princess, bride and beauty queen. No wonder so many young girls in Israel are called Ester or Esti. God picked this beautiful young girl to be the image of His plan for the human race. She is the image of the glorified Church bride standing next to Christ the King and ruling together with Him. What a powerful image!

Perhaps every Daddy sees his little girl as a princess. But God has lots of little girls, and they are all princesses in His eyes. Esther is the image of the princess. In that sense, she is a symbol of God's destiny for Israel, for the Church, for women and for the human race. She is a symbol of what God saw in Eve at the creation.

God has a vision for us to be like a glorified woman. That image runs throughout the Bible. It starts in Genesis, runs through the Song of Solomon and the book of Esther, all the way to the book of Revelation. **Revelation 12:1 – Now a great sign appeared in heaven: a woman clothed with the sun, with the moon under her feet, and on her head a garland of twelve stars.** This glorified woman of Revelation is a continuation of the glorified Zion from the prophets of Israel.

Isaiah 62:1-5
For Zion's sake I will not hold My peace, and for Jerusalem's sake I will not rest, until her righteousness goes forth as brightness...

You shall be a crown of glory in the hand of the Lord, and a royal diadem in the hand of your God...

You shall be called Delightful One and your land Married; for the Lord delights in you, and your land shall be married.

For as a young man marries a virgin, so shall your sons marry you; and as the bridegroom rejoices over the bride, so shall your God rejoice over you.

The biblical idea of a glorified bride develops and expands from the image of "Zion" in the Israelite prophets to the international "Ecclesia" of the New Covenant. But it is the same promise, the same prophecy, the same destiny. The people of God will be glorified with shining glorious bodies in the resurrection. They will be married to God. They will rule the universe together with Messiah Yeshua. God's purposes for both Israel and the Church will become one.

Beautiful and glorified, Queen Esther is the symbol of that destiny for all of us.

Each one of us has a destiny to be "glorified." Ultimately that means to have a resurrection body that shines like the sun (**I Corinthians 15:40-43**). The process of our salvation begins with repentance and forgiveness and ends up in being glorified in the likeness of Yeshua after a process of our being foreknown, predestined, called, justified and sanctified (**Romans 8:29-30**).

This is another secret mystery of God's plan. The Holy Spirit can reveal to us that God desires to "glorify" us (**I Corinthians 2:8**). Yeshua will return in glory (**Matthew 25:31**), and we will be like Him (**I John 3:1**). Our lowly bodies will be changed into glorious ones (**Philippians 3:21**). Even today we can by faith be transformed day by day more into the image of Yeshua in glory (**II Corinthians 3:18**).

Let us remind ourselves that the Church is a multi-national group of people. It is composed of the remnant of faith in each nation. Each has its own identity and expression within the overall international body. These are people who each have been "called out" in the midst of their nation to be part of the believing remnant of their nation and part of the international ecclesia of "called out" ones. The word ecclesia in Greek means just that, the "called out" ones.

The first nation to have a believing remnant was the nation of Israel. The ecclesia started there. The gospel message of the Kingdom is going around the world, and today there is a growing ecclesia in every nation. In the end the gospel will come back to Israel where it started. The restoration of the first remnant will be the last stage of the international ecclesia. The first will also be the last.

So on the one hand, the destiny of the Church is to be the glorious international ecclesia bride. Yet at the same time, the Church also has Jewish roots. The Church starts and ends with Israel. Many do not want to hear about that connection, whether on the Church side or the Israel side. However, the existence of the Messianic Jewish remnant in Israel today is forcing the issue. We are the bridge between the two. We are fully part of Israel and we are fully part of the international Church-ecclesia.

Amazingly enough, the same was true for Queen Esther. She was living in glory in the king's palace. She had servant girls. She had intimacy with the king. Yet at the same time, she had Jewish roots. She was born as a Jewish girl, and even if she tried to hide it, the truth had to come out in the end.

I think of Jane Hansen Hoyt of Aglow International, as a particularly appropriate image of Queen Esther in our day. All of Aglow, with hundreds of thousands of women worldwide that are worshipping the Lord and filled with the Holy Spirit, is quite an example of the Church as the glorified bride of Christ.

One day as we were praying for Jane, the prophetic image came forth of her and Aglow being like Esther, not only in the aspect of the glorified bride of Christ, but also in the "Jewish roots." The Israel part of the mandate of Aglow is just as central as their mandate for men and women. The image of the glorified bride and the acknowledgement of Jewish roots go together.

The desire to see the bride glorified should also affect the relationship between men and women in marriage. Men often want to emphasize their authority over the women in marriage. But the question should be asked, "What is that authority for?" It is for love, protection, provision, prayer and mutual dominion. It is also for causing the wife to be glorified. **That He might present her to Himself a glorious church – Ephesians 5:27.** The husband's job is to dedicate himself to see his wife reach all her glory, beauty and purity. He is to nurture her to become a glorious princess. A well-known quip of rabbis at Jewish weddings is: "If you want your wife to treat you as a king, treat her as a queen."

Esther is a great image of glory and beauty. Although the book of Esther describes real historical events that took place in the past, it also serves as a pattern for events yet to come in the end times. Soon we will also see an international evil empire that will try to kill Israel, all the Jews and all the Christians who will stand with them. Similar events as those that took place in Esther's time will take place again.

Most likely, Christians around the world will be faced with a choice. They can be identified with Israel and the Jews and thereby risk their lives with them. Or they can try to deny the connection in an effort to flee from the coming anti-Semitic genocide. This was exactly the same choice that Esther herself was faced with. Would she try to hide and deny her Jewish roots, or would she stand to intercede and be identified with her people?

The Church is like a beautiful Queen who has hidden Jewish roots.

At times I felt like a bit of a Mordecai toward Jane and Aglow, telling them they were called to stand with the Jewish people in the end times, no matter how difficult that tribulation might be and no matter how great the cost would be to stand with Israel. And how well they have done that! I have seen them don yellow stars of David, as in the Holocaust, in order to say, "should there come another Holocaust, we will stand with the Jewish people." Jane herself has been given awards of honor by the Israeli government and Israeli press.

Esther 4:13-14 – And Mordecai said in reply to Esther, "Do not imagine in your soul to escape in the king's house from the fate of all the Jews. For if you surely are silent at this time, peace and salvation will arise for the Jews from another place, but you and your father's house will perish. And who knows if for this time you have arrived at the kingdom?"

Esther's willingness to identify with the Jewish people and to stand with them in the midst of tribulation and potential genocide was part of her training and qualifying process to rule and reign beside the king over the whole world. So is it true, not only for Jane and Aglow, but also for the entire international Church. They are called to rule and reign with Christ; but part of the process to take hold of the Kingdom is standing by God's covenant with the Jewish people.

[As part of this calling to joint intercession in the image of Esther, we have organized for many years an international day of prayer and fasting coinciding with the traditional Jewish day of Esther's fast, "Ta'anit Ester". This is a 12 hour assembly for prayer, praise, prophecy and fasting. It is led by various local leaders and worship teams from different congregations throughout Israel. The central meeting takes place at Yad Hashmonah, the Messianic kibbutz on the outskirts of Jerusalem.

Most of the assembly with worship and intercession takes place in Hebrew, but we translate into English on the internet live stream broadcast. You are welcomed along with others in many nations to join us for that day. We publish the program and the list of prayer topics on the internet ahead of time in order to make it easier for our friends around the world to participate.]

Let us walk in the image of Esther, the glorified Bride, ruling and reigning with the King, and interceding for her Jewish people in times of trouble.

2

The Virgin Miriam

GIVING BIRTH TO
THE MESSIAH
(LUKE 1:26-56; 2:1-19)

From the very beginning of Scriptures, we find a cosmic conflict. God had delegated authority over planet earth to Adam and Eve (**Genesis 1:26; Psalm 8:6, 115:16**). One of the highest angels, Lucifer, became jealous and went down to earth to tempt them and thus became Satan, the enemy (**Genesis 3, Isaiah 14:12-20, Ezekiel 28:1-19**). Through sin, Satan usurped Adam's authority and took control over this world (**Luke 4:6, John 12:31, II Corinthians 4:4**). God countered with His plan to redeem the descendants of Adam and Eve and regain control of His creation.

Actually, God's plan did not seem on the surface to be so effective. He said that one day He would bring **"the seed of** the woman to crush the head of the serpent" – Genesis 3:15. Well, the serpent was Satan. The woman would be Eve herself or a female descendant in her place. The seed would be a man, a righteous man who would come from the woman and defeat Satan. Since Satan deceived Eve, God would "deceive" Satan in return through one of the woman's descendants. Since God gave authority to Adam, it would be a male descendant of Adam who would take back that lost authority. God's plan would be reciprocal and righteous.

So far, so good. However, it didn't seem so good. It seemed too easy for Satan to tempt into sin anyone who was open to sin or kill anyone who tried to be righteous. Adam and Eve had two sons, Cain (Kayin) and Abel (Hevel). Abel seemed to be good, and Cain seemed to be bad. It seemed obvious that Abel was the prophesied seed, and Cain was the serpent's seed. So Satan simply influenced Cain to kill Abel. Game over. Satan wins; God and mankind lose.

But God did not give up. He replaced Abel with another seed son, Seth. The name Seth (or "Shet") means to establish or set in place. Notice the very exact wording of **Genesis 4:25 – And the woman gave birth to a son and called his name "Seth" for God has "set" for me another seed in place of Abel whom Cain killed.** This was the continuance of the prophecy of the Messianic seed from **Genesis 3:15.**

So continues the spiritual history of man. Satan seems to be able to quite easily tempt men to sin or to kill them. Satan's plan is simple and brilliant: "tempt the sinners; murder the saints." God's plan seems helpless and hopeless, but God keeps going. In some ways, all of history may be seen as God's attempt to get this seed born into the world and Satan's attempt to thwart it.

The conflict goes on for centuries:

- All of **Noah**'s generation is cut off leaving only his family (a descendant of Seth) to bring the seed into the world **(Genesis 6)**

- God finds a righteous man in **Abraham** and cuts covenant with him that the seed will only come from his sons. At that point Satan disregards every other person in the world and focuses his efforts to destroy Abraham and his family **(Genesis 12)**

- Abraham stupidly gives his wife to other men **(Genesis 12:13; 20:1)**

- **Sarah** foolishly gives her handmaiden to Abraham **(Genesis 16)**

- The sons of **Ishmael** and **Esau** later try to kill the sons of Isaac and Jacob

- God makes a covenant with **Judah** that the seed will come through him **(Genesis 49:10)**

- **Pharaoh** tries to kill all the seed in Egypt **(Exodus 1)**

- The descendants of **Israel** are plagued with sexual immorality, jealousy and violence from within and without

- The covenant with Judah is extended to **David**, so that the eternal Messianic King must come from David's seed

- The evil queens **Jezebel** and **Athalia** try to kill all children and grandchildren who are the sons of David **(II Kings 11:1-3)**

- **Haman** tries to kill all the seed in Persia **(Esther 3)**

- In the time of **Ezra** and **Nehemiah**, the returning remnant intermarries with pagan Canaanite women and again endangers the seed **(Ezra 9:1-2)**

- By the time we get to the New Covenant period, **Herod** kills all the children in Bethlehem after hearing the prophecy of the wise men from the East **(Matthew 2)**

[These are just a very few examples. Much of the history of the Mosaic Law and the Hebraic Prophets can be understood as a battle to corrupt the seed by sexual sin or to kill it by murderous attack. Hence the two strongest of the Ten Commandments, "Thou shalt not murder; thou shalt not commit adultery" – **Exodus 20:13-14]**.

Finally, against all odds, the Messianic seed that will crush the head of Satan as prophesied in **Genesis 3:15** was indeed born into the world. The birth of this seed was the fulfillment of the Genesis prophecy. It was also a great victory for the human race in general and the Jewish people in particular. In some ways the birth of Yeshua, the Messianic seed, could be considered as the crowning event of Jewish history and the greatest of all Jewish Holy Days.

That birth, by the grace of God, overcame the acts of the serpent to prevent it and completed the first major stage of the plan of God. This great fulfillment of prophecy about the Messianic seed and the covenant destiny of the Jewish people required a "woman." The Messiah is the seed of "the woman."

It had to be someone. It had to be a real person. It had to be a descendant of David. It had to be a girl who maintained her sexual purity in the midst of a lustful world. It had to be a girl who would believe in the supernatural power of God to fulfill His promises. It had to be a woman who would be willing to sacrifice her life, reputation and body for the sake of the Kingdom of God.

There was such a woman. Her name is Miriam. She is known to the world as Mary, Mother Mary, the real Madonna. While we totally disagree with her deification and her "gentilization," we should at the same time recognize her as a great heroine of the faith. She is the Jewish virgin. She fulfilled Messianic prophecies from Genesis to Isaiah to Micah. She is one of the greatest women of faith in the history of Israel.

She did it. She believed. This daughter of Sarah, Rebekah and Leah; this daughter of King David; this pure-hearted young woman beat the devil and fulfilled the prophecies for the redemption of the human race. I think she needs to be "re-adopted" by the Jewish people and by the Evangelical and Charismatic churches. (She never did convert to Catholicism; although it is the Catholics who have most appreciated her role in history.)

In translating her name from Miriam to Mary, the historical connection with Miriam the sister of Moses is lost, as well as the prophetic connection to the covenants of the Jewish people. It's interesting to note that so many of Yeshua's women disciples in the first century were called "Miriam" (again translated to Mary).

It seems to me that many of them identified with the image of that first Miriam. She was the one who saved Moses from Pharaoh (**Exodus 2:4-9**), was the first known prophetess in the Bible, and led the daughters of Israel in the first worship and praise dance celebration with tambourine in hand (**Exodus 15:20**). Ah, how many of our spiritual sisters can identify with that today: saving children, prophesying and worshiping in dance!

Where Eve failed and yielded to the devil, Miriam (the mother of Yeshua) — the great, great… granddaughter of Eve – succeeded. She overcame the devil. This daughter of Eve fulfilled the promise of God to Eve. Miriam's faith and purity is a partial reversal of Eve's sin and deception. She gave birth to the King Messiah.

It is worth noting that Miriam's job, like any mother, did not end at birth, it just started. It was her responsibility to raise this unusual child. This was not an easy task, and she did not always do it perfectly. She worried about Him (**Luke 2:48**) and even thought He had gone insane at one point (**Mark 3:21, 31**). But it was she who gave Him the sign to start the miracle-working aspect of His ministry (**John 2:3-11**).

As any mother knows, it is an extremely painful process to raise children. As the elderly Simeon prophesied over her, **"and a sword will pass through your heart, in order that the thoughts of many will be revealed"** – Luke 2:35. This piercing of the sword in her heart was not referring to the birth pains but to the spiritual and emotional challenges of being the mother of the savior of the world.

[Interestingly enough, the Jewish aspect of the "Virgin Mary" has been the source of some rather disrespectful humor in Israel, albeit funny. Perhaps that's because of the famous obsessive-neurotic relationships between Jewish mothers and their sons. "How do you know Jesus was Jewish? He was thirty years old and still thought his mom was a virgin; and she… well, she thought he was God Himself!"

Personally, I cannot help thinking that when Miriam comes to Yeshua after He "ran away from home" so-to-speak as a twelve-year old, and says to Him (**Luke 2:48** *paraphrased*), "How could you do this to us? Don't you know how worried we were?" – had to be one of the most humorous and "Jewish" aspects of the Gospels. (*Or, do you have to be Jewish to know what is funny about that?*)]

The prophecy of the seed of the woman from **Genesis 3:15** refers first to Miriam, but it is expanded to all the godly women in Israel and the Church who have suffered, loved and sacrificed to raise godly children in an ungodly world. Every mother is attacked by the devil for trying to raise her children correctly in love and righteousness.

When Yeshua was born, all the children in Bethlehem were murdered. That event is described as a fulfillment of the prophecy about the New Covenant from the book of Jeremiah. **A voice was heard in Ramah, Lamentation and bitter weeping, Rachel weeping for her children, refusing to be comforted – Jeremiah 31:15; Matthew 2:18.** Rachel, Miriam, the mothers of Bethlehem, the mothers in the book of **Lamentations 2:18-19**, and all godly mothers who have wept and prayed and cared for their children in the midst of an evil world are all of the same spirit.

Prayer and intercession is seen as a type of child birth and labor. **My little children, for whom I labor again in birth until Christ is formed within you… - Galatians 4:19.** May we all dedicate ourselves to pray and care for the spiritual and physical children in our generation!

I want to dedicate this chapter to all those godly mothers. There is not one who has not been attacked spiritually. There is not one who has not felt the pain of a spiritual sword cutting through her heart and emotions. To be a mother is to sacrifice one's body on a daily basis. It is to take up the cross every day. These are the unsung heroines of the Kingdom of God.

These are all the daughters of Miriam. May they see the fruit of their labors (**Proverbs 31:31**) and receive their eternal reward!

Being a good dad or mom today is an enormous challenge. It is a painful job. Let us commit ourselves to see this generation of parents arise with godly wisdom, faith, patience and sacrifice to raise a generation of children, natural and spiritual, who may well be those to welcome the return of the Messiah.

Miriam won the battle by God's grace and fulfilled the first great Messianic prophecy from **Genesis 3:15** about the seed of the woman defeating the serpent. However, that spiritual battle continues today and will continue into the future. It is a cosmic and universal battle for every generation that is parallel to the specific battle over the birth of Yeshua through Miriam.

Revelation 12:2-4 – Then being with child, she cried out in labor and in pain to give birth. And another sign appeared in heaven: behold a great, fiery red dragon... stood before the woman who was ready to give birth, to devour her child as soon as it was born.

This passage has multiple meanings. It is about Yeshua and Miriam, but also about all godly mothers and sons. It is past, present and future.

One might have thought that when Yeshua was born, all the meaning of the Messianic seed prophecy was fulfilled and that the covenant destiny of the Jewish people ended at that time. It is possible to see the logic in that view point. The problem is that

Yeshua made a statement about the future of the Jewish people. They were to be integrally involved not only in His first coming but in His second coming as well.

Matthew 23:37-39 – O Jerusalem, Jerusalem, the one who kills the prophets and stones those who are sent to her! How often I wanted to gather your children together as a hen gathers her chicks under her wings, but you were not willing! See, your house is left to you desolate; for I say to you, you will not see Me again until you say, "Blessed is He who comes in the name of the Lord!"

This is an amazing statement that has earth-shaking and history-changing implications. Yeshua not only predicted the destruction of the Second Temple, He said that the faith of the Jews in Jerusalem was a prerequisite to the Second Coming.

I have often pondered ironically if this was a strategic mistake on Yeshua's part. After all, our people certainly seemed to have given God enough problems over history. Wouldn't it have been much simpler, much cleaner and much easier to have said that Yeshua will come back when a certain number of people in the future from any nation of the world would believe in Him and invite Him to return?

That certainly would have been a much more "universal" approach. However, God's approach is both universal and covenantal. Yes, salvation and the Kingdom of God are open to everyone. The Church-ecclesia is perfectly universal. Yet at the same time, God respects His past covenants and commitments.

Israel is His family. After all the history of His faithfulness to the people of Israel, is He going to abandon them in the end times? Certainly not!

So as Miriam gave birth to Yeshua's first coming, there will be a Messianic remnant and a national revival in Israel that will "give birth" to His second coming. We all have a role to play in praying and preparing this Messianic seed generation to arise. It is an equal calling for all Christians of every nation, as well as the prophesied coming seed in Jerusalem. Just as there was an intense spiritual battle over the First Coming, so will there be an equal if not greater spiritual battle over the Second Coming.

Let us take our role to be a company of "Miriams". Let us identify with Miriam and give birth to the Messianic Kingdom in our generation just as she gave birth to the Messianic King in her generation.

A last word should be spoken about her purity. While I do not believe that Miriam herself was born "immaculately," I do greatly respect her commitment to sexual purity. She was a virgin. I imagine she was a pretty young girl, sought after, and had to confront temptations of the flesh like any other human being.

When the angel Gabriel came to Zechariah, the father of John the Baptist, Zechariah expressed unbelief that a son could be born to his aged wife. He was punished for this unbelief by being unable to talk for nine months (**Luke 1:18-20**).

When the angel Gabriel then came to Miriam to tell her about the birth of Yeshua, she asked what seemed to be a similar question, **"How could this be, since I do not know a man?" – Luke 1:34.** For this Miriam was not punished but rather received an explanation from the angel as to how it would happen.

While Miriam's and Zechariah's questions seem somewhat similar, they were totally different in nature. Zechariah was questioning God's **power.** How could this happen? Miriam was defending her own **purity.** She did not and does not have relations with a man. She would fight for her holiness even before an angel. "I do not and will not compromise on my purity. So how do you expect this to happen? I know God can do anything, but I also know that I am to guard my virginity at all costs, even unto death, whether before men or angels."

Here, I imagine that Gabriel did not frown as he likely did with Zechariah but smiled at her determination and holiness. Perhaps that determination had been tested before by other young men in the town. Perhaps she had said "No" before as she now said "No" to Gabriel. Her humility and purity were part of her qualifications to be the virgin maiden who would bring the savior into the world.

Let's not forget that Miriam was the great, great… granddaughter of King David. Remember all the incidents of sexual immorality that had plagued their family for generations. Miriam refused to give into that curse. She held the line of purity for King Messiah, the greater son of David, to be born in a holy and miraculous way.

Thank you, Miriam.

Supplement: Was Miriam a Virgin?

Those who know biblical Hebrew well are aware that the prophecy in Isaiah 7 about the birth of "Immanuel" – God with us – through a virgin, does not use the normal word for virgin, "Bethulah" בתולה , but another word "Almah" עלמה . This is a very special word that is used three times in biblical prophecy.

Miriam was not a normal virgin. She was a betrothed virgin. She would have had to go through a divorce to separate from Joseph. She was legally his wife even though they had not been together physically.

This "betrothed" situation was necessary for Yeshua to be born legally as the son of Joseph, and also to be physically born of a miracle of the Holy Spirit. A normal wife could not have fulfilled the prophecies, because she would have had physical relations with her husband. A normal virgin could not have fulfilled the prophecies because she would have no legal husband. She had to be in that double category of a virgin physically but married physically.

That is why the Torah had a special provision for betrothal and a special category of a virgin betrothed. It had to be a different category and that is why a different word is used. As a virgin betrothed, she would have been stoned to death had she committed adultery (**Deuteronomy 22:23-24**). It is for this reason that Joseph sought to divorce her secretly (**Matthew 1:19**).

The first time "Almah" is used refers to Rebekah. She was Miriam's great, great… grandmother. In **Genesis 24:16** she is referred to as a virgin "bethulah" and in **Genesis 24:43** as "almah." So almah and bethulah both refer to a virgin. The mother of the Messiah had to be a descendant of Rebekah and a virgin, both almah and bethulah.

Almah is found a second time in **Exodus 2:8** referring to Miriam the sister of Moses, as a foreshadow of Miriam the mother of Yeshua. So, the future mother of Messiah would be called almah and be called Miriam. They would have the same name.

The third time is of course **Isaiah 7:14** where the almah will give birth to the messianic king, a supernatural child, born as a miraculous sign; and, that child will be called Immanuel - God with us.

So let's put the three incidents together to see the mystery of the prophetic puzzle:

1. An almah who is a virgin and a descendant of Rebekah (**Genesis 24**),

2. Whose name will be Miriam (**Exodus 2**),

3. Will give birth in a miraculous way to a baby who will be called, "God With Us" (**Isaiah 7:14**).

3

The Canaanite Woman

CRUMBS OF HEALING
FOR OUR CHILDREN
(MATTHEW 15:21-28, MARK 7:24-30)

Similar to the faith and humility of Miriam is that of a woman from a totally different background: the "Canaanite woman" from Matthew 15 and Mark 7. Yeshua and His disciples were walking in the area of Tyre and Sidon near the border of Southern Lebanon. Yeshua was looking for a time of quiet and tried to hide their presence, but word got out that they were there.

A woman, described as of Canaanite background in Matthew or Phoenician in Mark, finds them and falls at Yeshua's feet and cries aloud begging that He would heal her daughter. To what degree she was genealogically a Canaanite or a Phoenician is not important here. What is significant is that she had such an identity in the eyes of the Jewish disciples of Yeshua and possibly even to Yeshua Himself. She was a Gentile. If she was a Canaanite, then she was born of a cursed racial background.

In other words, not only is there the challenge of her daughter's illness, there is also the problem of her own identity in the face of racial discrimination, religious prejudice and social rejection. How does this woman even dare to come ask the "King of the Jews" a request? There does not seem to be any chance that He would relate to her at all. (The Matthew version emphasizes the racial issues more than Mark, who perhaps "softened" it later. But for our purposes, we want to take note of those psychological and social problems.)

Yeshua hears faith in her voice. But He also senses something is wrong. Perhaps there is something wrong in her own self-image; perhaps it is in the discriminatory attitude of His own disciples; perhaps both. So He has to deal with both of those problems before turning to the healing of the daughter.

Yeshua's disciples rather unkindly request from Yeshua to "get rid of her" as she is bothering them. He decides to hit all the issues head on, and says, **"I was not sent except to the lost sheep of the house of Israel" – Matthew 15:24.**

[This was a true statement. Yeshua only widened the message of the Kingdom to the Gentiles after the time of His resurrection (**John 12:20-23; Acts 1:8**). In the gospels and Yeshua's lifetime (on earth), the ministry was only to Israel (**Matthew 10:5-6; 15:24**). After Yeshua ascended to heaven, the disciples received the Holy Spirit. Only then did they begin to spread the message to other nations. However, in the case of the "Canaanite" woman, Yeshua recognized that an exception to the general pattern was taking place (as with the Samaritan woman in **John 4**). Perhaps Yeshua was even surprised Himself.]

In light of this complex social situation, we can understand the passage as Yeshua challenging the woman to rise to even a higher measure of faith and challenging the disciples to lower their racial pride. The whole incident is taking place on two "levels" at the same time.

The woman responds with a persistent and desperate faith. **Matthew 15:25 – She came closer and fell down before Him and said, "Lord, Help me!"** We can imagine how deeply this is touching Yeshua's heart of compassion, yet He wants to "raise the bar" (or "lower the bar") to even a greater level. He pushes the issue all the way. **Matthew 15:26 - It is not right to take the children's bread and give it to the dogs.** Ouch!

Yeshua calls her a dog. He refers to all Gentiles here as dogs. He refers to His Jewish disciples as "children of the Kingdom" and the Gentiles as illegitimate. He is pushing everyone's understanding "off the edge." Perhaps there is a moment of awkward silence. Then the woman says, **"Yes, Lord, but even the dogs eat the crumbs falling from their masters' table" – verse 27.**

This is a spiritual explosion of historic proportions. The woman's faith in Yeshua, her own humility and her relentless love for her daughter breaks through all the walls of unbelief and prejudice on every side and, perhaps, even the time dispensations of the plan of God. Her faith is changing historic patterns. I can imagine Yeshua smiling (both with relief and pride) and thinking to Himself, "You did it. Way to go, girl!"

He replies, **"Woman, great is your faith. It will be done to you according to your will," and from that very hour her child was healed – verse 28.** The humility and love in this woman caused a breakthrough of the Kingdom for the Gentiles long before it was due to happen in the leadership of Peter and Paul. Her faith overcame all obstacles – personal, physical, family, cultural, social and religious.

It is important to note that this Gentile woman was not asking for healing for herself but for her daughter. Her tenacious faith was for a family member. Let us look at this incident in the perspective of a parent praying for his or her family.

The world is in a crisis concerning family values. There is a breakdown of the nuclear family as never before in history. This is a curse spreading across the world. The last prophet of the Hebrew Scriptures is Malachi. The last verse of his prophecy deals with just this – the breakdown of the family in the generation of the end times.

Malachi 4:5-6
Behold I send you Elijah the prophet before the coming of the great and terrible day of YHVH; and he will turn the hearts of the fathers to the children; and the hearts of the children to their fathers, lest I come and strike the earth with a curse.

I do not believe that this passage is referring to a personal return of Elijah himself but to a renewed prophetic ministry and revelation in a similar anointing to that of Elijah (just as John the Baptist prophesied in the same **"spirit and power of Elijah"** - **Matthew 11:14, Luke 1:17**).

Notice the timing of the last days; notice the issue of parental-child breakdown; notice the worldwide dimension; notice the spirit of prophecy healing the situation. This is one of the most urgent issues of our generation.

There is an order: first the fathers to the children, and then the children to the fathers. It is for the parents to take the initiative. If they do, the Scriptures promise that the children will return in kind. We can see the Canaanite woman as a model for this healing of the generations.

First of all, she has to humble herself – even humbling herself to the point of crawling on the ground, likening herself to a dog and being shamed in front of others. But that does not deter her. Sometimes to reach the heart of our children, we have to go through some rather humiliating experiences.

The word for "turn the hearts" in Hebrew reminds me of the phrase for turning one's attention, getting one's attention. The fathers have to turn the attention of their hearts to the spiritual situation of their children.

One woman in our Jerusalem congregation had a dream about the leaders of the community being involved in steering a large boat. But as they were steering the boat, the children were playing in the back of the ship, and many of them started falling into the water without being noticed. Once in the water, they were in mortal danger of drowning and shark attack. We may have to go jump off the boat into the water in order to go find and save our children and their generation.

As spiritual leaders and as parents, we are faced with an urgent situation to turn the attention of our hearts to our children. We must humble ourselves, turn our attention to them, listen to what is on their hearts, and then God can heal them.

The healing of the children is likened to crumbs of bread; each child needs a crumb of bread. I imagine a crumb is like the size of a mustard seed. One crumb-seed size of faith can move a mountain (**Matthew 17:20**) or it can heal a child (**Matthew 15:27**). Let's do everything we need to do to acquire and release those healing crumbs for our children and families. Let our faith break through every social and cultural barrier as well.

The turning of hearts goes first from the fathers to children, and then from the children to fathers. If we compare this to the teaching of the Ten Commandments, we will see that these two directions apply not only to one generation but to three or four.

Deuteronomy 5:9 – visiting the sins of the fathers upon the children unto the third and fourth generations of those who hate Me.

The chain of cause and effect goes to three or four generations. Yet this same syndrome of generational transfer can work in the positive for blessing much more powerfully than in the negative for curse. "Visiting the sins" is the curse (verse 9). The blessing is described in the next verse:

Deuteronomy 5:10 – and acting in loving-kindness to those who love Me unto thousands.

The grace and loving-kindness is much stronger than the sin and the curse; the negative direction is for 3-4 generations, but the positive direction is for thousands. However, the pattern of generational transfer is the same. Let us summarize the pattern this way:

1. **Direction** – up and down: parents to children; children to parents

2. **Order** – parents first, then children

3. **Promise** - if parents turn, then the children will turn

4. **Multi-generational** – to three and four generations the healing is needed

5. **Positive or negative** – sins and curses can transfer and so can blessings and healing.

The rule is that there is always cause and effect. What we sow, we reap. What we do to others eventually "comes around." God enforces His own rules of cause and effect.

When we are young, we do not realize how we are acting towards our parents. We are too self-centered. As we have children, we recognize in them ways in which we acted to our parents. When our children are babies, we understand the investment of our parents in us as babies. When our children are teenagers, we recognize how we acted as teens. When they are adults and we are grandparents, we recognize how we treated our older parents.

This pattern allows us an opportunity to reverse the curse at every and any age. We can change the pattern by "turning our hearts." This brings healing up and down the line in both directions to parents and grandparents and to children and grandchildren.

Recently I watched a movie about World War I. The line of battle between Russia and Germany was in the area of Ukraine and Poland called Galicia. That is where my great grandparents lived. After the war, my grandfather immigrated to the United States. Most of his relatives who stayed in that area were murdered in World War II.

[Auschwitz is located in that area. Many of the generation of my great grandparents were killed in that area. January, 2015 marked the 70th year anniversary of the liberating of Auschwitz. The 70 year period is a biblical period for the fulfillment of a curse and punishment. It also represents the promised life span (**Psalm 90:10**). It coincides with the previous 2nd and 3rd generations passing away. The year 2015 marked in the history of Israel the coming to an end of an era. Very few of the eyewitness Holocaust survivors remain. A new period of history has begun.]

I wonder how my great grandparents felt when their son left them to travel overseas. I wonder how my grandparents (Yiddish speaking) felt as my parents grew up in a new language and culture in America that they could never really join. I wonder how my parents felt when we immigrated to Israel when their grandchildren (our children) were born. How have my children felt growing up in this pioneer and war-torn country? May God bring a healing to all the parents and children of all peoples to three and four generations!

We need to exercise all the power we have in prayer and the Scriptures to bring about this generational healing. Here are some biblical promises to encourage our faith:

- God has made a covenant with us that our children and our children's children will follow in our faith (**Isaiah 59:21**).

- Our children will be like olive shoots around our table for family meals and fellowship (**Psalms 128:3**).

- They will be like arrows in our quiver to fight for our same values in the world around us (**Psalm 127:3-4**).

- Our children will have peace of mind and health in body (**Isaiah 54:13**).

- Our children will return to their boundaries, both physically and spiritually (**Jeremiah 31:17**).

- We can rescue everything of our families like David did at Ziklag (**I Samuel 30:19**).

- For whatever the devil has destroyed, we can get a double return like Job (**Job 42:10**).

- For those who fear the Lord, our children will fulfill a great and mighty destiny on earth (**Psalm 112:2**).

- It will be great joy to hear that our children are walking in truth (**III John 4**).

- God will turn the hearts of our children like young kings and queens to Himself (**Proverbs 21:1**).

To turn the hearts of the parents and children demands humility and patience on both sides. One needs to be willing to crawl like a dog under the table, as it were, just like the Canaanite woman. We have to listen and to give time and attention.

May we be sensitive to one another's pains, to one another's feelings, to one another's hearts! May we be like the Canaanite/Phoenician woman who humbled herself, who fought tenaciously against all odds through faith and love in order to heal her daughter! May God give us the power and spirit of Elijah in our day to bring healing to our families across all generations!

4
The Sinful Woman
TOTAL DEPRAVITY AND DESPERATE LOVE
(LUKE 7:36-50)

One of the Jewish religious leaders named Shimon (Simeon) invited Yeshua to dine at his home. At that time a "sinful woman" from the city, who heard that Yeshua was there, snuck into the house and came up to Yeshua from behind. She knelt down at His feet and wept. She washed His feet with her tears, wiped them dry with her hair, kissed His feet and then poured perfume upon them.

Simeon and Yeshua saw the event from entirely different angles. Simeon saw it as degrading, carnal and bordering on sinful. He also thought that it showed how unperceptive Yeshua was in not recognizing how sinful the woman was. Yeshua on the other hand saw the event as an uncommon expression of repentance, love and dedication on the woman's part.

Yeshua told a story about two debtors, one who owed 500 dinars and one 50. If they were both forgiven, who would be more thankful? Simeon answered correctly that the one who owed more would be more thankful and therefore more loving in return. Yeshua saw this woman's reaction as an expression of deep gratitude and love for knowing that her debt of sin, though great, had been forgiven by Yeshua.

Luke 7:44-47
Do you see this woman? I came into your house and you gave me no water for My feet, yet she with her tears has washed My feet and with her hair has dried them. You gave Me no kiss, yet she since I came in has not stopped kissing My feet. You did not anoint My head with oil, yet she with perfume has anointed My feet. Therefore I say to you, her many sins are forgiven her because of the greatness of her love. But he who is forgiven little, loves little.

The foundation of all spiritual life is repentance, true repentance. Jeremiah said that repentance was the central message of all of the prophets of Israel (**Jeremiah 25:4-5**). When Yeshua began His teaching ministry, He called for repentance (**Matthew 4:17**). When Peter (Shimon Kefa) preached the gospel, he started with repentance (**Acts 2:38**). When Paul preached to the Gentiles, he explained that God is calling every person in the whole world to repent (**Acts 17:30**).

Repentance means being aware that we have done wrong, admitting it, asking forgiveness and committing to do what is right. When forgiven, repentance should be accompanied by a deep expression of gratitude.

Although many speak of repentance, it seems to me that real repentance is quite rare. In both Judaism and Christianity, we make spiritual excuses which cover up our lack of real heart repentance. Tradition replaces repentance. In Judaism that tradition is in ritual law. In Christianity that tradition is in theology. Actually, making excuses for wrongdoing, instead of confessing and repenting, started long before Judaism or Christianity: it started all the way back in the Garden of Eden (**Genesis 3:12-13**).

In rabbinic Judaism, repentance is mentioned quite often, but it normally means to make a commitment to do a set of ritual laws ("Halacha" הלכה) and not really to seek to change by recognizing the depth of moral sin. In Western Christianity, there is often an overlooking of repentance altogether by making humanistic excuses and believing that only a superficial affirmation of Christ will result in eternal salvation and spiritual transformation.

Where can we find a case of true repentance? What examples do we have in real life, or even in the Bible? Perhaps the people of Israel at the time of receiving the Torah at Mount Sinai (**Exodus 19**). Or the people of Nineveh responding to the preaching of Jonah (**Jonah 1**). As a personal expression of repentance, the reaction of David after the sin with Bat-Sheva stands out in its sincerity and depth (**Psalm 51**).

Most of the time, David was a man with an extremely sensitive conscience. Once, his heart struck him with guilt even for having cut off the hem of King Saul's garment (**I Samuel 24:6**). It is amazing that he could have been so sensitive to his conscience toward Saul at the time that Saul was trying to kill him. David repented even though his men were unanimous in demanding him to kill Saul. David heard the whispered demands of his own conscience above the "noise" of the circumstances around him.

Equally amazing was that David was as insensitive to his conscience in the situation with Bat-Sheva as he was sensitive in the case of Saul. In the lures of lust, David did not hear his own heart reprimanding him at the time of the sin with Bat-Sheva. He openly murdered, lied and committed adultery and then covered it up with hypocrisy. However, after the prophet Nathan rebuked him, David repented to the depths of his heart.

David killed the giant Goliath without any weapons by his victorious faith. But the girl Bat-Sheva knocked David down without any weapons at all. What King Saul could not do with swords and spears, Bat-Sheva did with only a bath towel. [My wife and I agree on almost everything in the Bible except for this point. I claim that Bat-Sheva flirted and enticed David on purpose; my wife claims she was innocently abducted, taken by David's lust. Likely my wife is correct.]

In any case, there was an even greater challenge to deal with for David, more than Goliath, Saul and Bat-Sheva together – the need to repent and to receive forgiveness. How is it that God in His sovereignty allowed for this whole incident to take place with Bat-Sheva bathing in front of the king's window and Uriyah refusing to go home to sleep with his wife? It seems that it was to allow David to experience the depth of sin and repentance and to record his feelings in the Bible afterward.

It also seems from the text that it was not David alone who had a problem with lust and adultery, but that sexual sins were found commonly across the nation. For that reason the sin had to be revealed and punished publicly. It was a warning to everyone.

While David did not repent during his adultery, murder and lying, he certainly did repent when he was rebuked for his sin by the prophet Nathan. Out of that experience came the poignant cry of Psalm 51, which has been the foremost expression of heartfelt repentance in history. **"Create in me a pure heart, O God; and renew a right spirit within me. Do not cast me away from your presence, and do not take your Holy Spirit from me"** – **Psalm 51:11-12.** Who has not been touched by these words?

David's repentance after his sin with Bat-Sheva was a greater spiritual breakthrough than his victory over Goliath and King Saul. (It also took great faith for David, after repenting of his sin and the death of their son, to be reunited with Bat-Sheva and believe for God to restore their destiny and continue with His plan for their lives. Perhaps both Bat-Sheva and the "sinful woman" of Luke 7 had similar feelings of guilt to overcome in that regard.)

Here's a little Bible quiz: Which of the kings of Israel ruled the longest number of years? The answer is Menashe (Manasseh) who ruled 55 years. Manasseh was one of the most sinful kings of Judah, and because of his sins, the final judgment of destruction and exile came upon Jerusalem. He was involved in corruption, pagan worship, child sacrifice, murder and immorality. Why then did God allow him to rule for so long?

God sent the Assyrian army into Israel, and had Manasseh captured and put in jail in chains. While he was in jail, he repented deeply. **"And when he was in tribulation, he sought the face of YHVH his God, and humbled himself greatly before the God of his fathers" – II Chronicles 33:12.** Because of the depth of that repentance, he was released from jail and sought moral and religious reform.

God waited all that time to allow Manasseh the opportunity to repent. The 55 years were a demonstration of the amazing patience and grace of God. (However, it was still not enough to stop the eventual punishment for the entire nation a generation later.)

While we can be touched by the repentance of David and of Manasseh, there is something about the "sinful woman" of Luke 7 that goes to a deeper level than any other example I can think of. She is the "ultimate" expression of repentance.

It seems to me that God "fore-knew" the sensitivity of this woman's heart, her willingness to recognize the depth of her own sin, and her ability to express that repentance in such a poignant way. Could it be that God destined her to be born in Yeshua's generation, allowed her to sin and then arranged for her the opportunity to be brought before Yeshua? If so, this woman, the human being who would show the greatest demonstration of personal repentance in all history, was "saved up" for this moment in time to express such a heart-felt repentance before the Messiah Himself.

And what a stunning moment it was! Like David's repentance in Psalm 51, her expression of devotion and contrition was recorded in the Bible for all to read for generations to come. I certainly identify with her and in some ways am even a bit jealous. You and I are no better than she was in her sin; yet, she seems much better than we are in her expression of devotion and repentance in response.

Yeshua said that one who is forgiven much loves much. Does that mean she sinned more than anyone else in history? I doubt it. She didn't seem to have committed murder, theft or rebellion. The impression from the passage is she committed some form of sexual immorality. We do not know. The point is that it is not necessarily the quantity of her sin but the depth of her being aware of it.

Shortly after I came to faith, I was struggling with feelings of guilt over previous sin. There was a young couple leading worship in the congregation. They were very nice looking and their worship was very pure. I went to them, told them of my struggle with guilt feelings, and asked them for counsel. The wife turned to me and said, "Oh, I can understand you, I struggle with similar feelings myself." I was stunned. I said, "No, I'm sure you never sinned; you're so pure." At that point they both laughed out loud.

As they laughed out loud, I was freed from a plaguing, "dark cloud" of self-condemnation.

Since we have all sinned, we find ourselves between two different "traps." On one hand is self-righteousness; on the other hand is self-condemnation. Yeshua told this woman she was totally forgiven. By His blood, we are cleansed of all guilt and condemnation (**Hebrews 9:14; I John 1:7**). There is a position of intimacy and grace with Yeshua in which we are totally repentant at the depth of our sinfulness, yet at the same time we are totally freed of any condemnation.

God's love is all in all to us. God's grace provides the solution for both self-righteousness and self-condemnation. Instead of being sinful, we can be holy; instead of being self-righteous, we can be humble; instead of being self-condemning, we can be healthy and whole.

We have all sinned. The question is whether we are willing to be aware of the depth of our sin. We have the tendency to see other's sins more than our own. We want to take the speck out of someone else's eye instead of taking the beam out of our own eye. **"Why do you see the speck in your brother's eye and do not see the beam in your own eye?" – Matthew 7:3.** It is hard for human beings to recognize their own faults, yet so easy to recognize the sins of others.

At the first sin of Adam and Eve in the Garden of Eden, both of them avoided repenting. Adam said it was Eve's fault; Eve said it was the devil's fault (**Genesis 3:10-13**). Certainly they themselves could not be to blame! They began the most fundamental of all human artwork: the subtle craftsmanship of blame shifting. It has continued to this day with rare exceptions.

In some ways, this sinful woman of **Luke 7** reversed the curse of sinful Eve. She broke the pattern of avoiding repentance started by Adam and Eve. Instead of making excuses, she repented with all her heart. The point is not how much this woman sinned. Her sin was not any worse to God than Simeon's, than Adam's or Eve's, than yours or mine. However, she repented at such a beautiful depth that Yeshua was touched by her tears and commended her.

Out of the depth of repentance came a depth of love. The greatest of all commandments is to love God with all our hearts (**Deuteronomy 6:5**). This woman fulfilled this great commandment in a great way, perhaps more than the most famous of religious leaders, Jewish and Christian alike.

Paul wrote that he was the **"greatest of all sinners"** – **I Timothy 1:15.** He also wrote that in his and our "flesh" resides **"no good thing"** – **Romans 7:18.** Throughout the Law and the Prophets are reminders that there is no one good before God.

At the Garden of Eden, the problem was not just that Adam and Eve sinned, but that they refused to repent afterwards. In some ways their self-justification and self-righteousness was more of a problem than the sin itself. This is an essential message of the grace of God in the Scriptures. Self-righteousness blocks the purposes of God just as much as sin. If we follow this woman's example, we will be free of that propensity to self-justification.

There is a certain paradox in our relationship with God. The more He expresses His power to us and through us, the more we realize that we have no power of ourselves. Where we are weak, He can be strong (**II Corinthians 12:10**). The more we grow in purity of motives, the more we see just how impure our motives have been. The closer we come to His holiness, the more we see our own depravity (**Isaiah 6:3, 5**).

Let us move into that intense and intimate place where we are overwhelmed by His holiness and our depravity. And in that moment, we are swept by His grace into a total experience of the love of God from the highest place to the lowest. It is a roller coaster ride of worship and adoration—the ultimate pleasure, an "extreme" sport. It is the experience of infinite and amazing grace. To the degree we can recognize the depth of our own depravity, we can also experience the height of devotional passion.

May we be like this woman! May we start each day with recognizing our own depravity and unworthiness! May we turn that recognition into a depth of gratefulness to God for His mercy and into a depth of dedication and devotion to purity! May we love God with every bit of our heart, soul and strength!

The purpose of repentance is recognition of reality. It is not to wallow in guilt, self-condemnation or self-pity. It is to launch us into greater love. Let us walk in the same love as that sinful woman, so that Yeshua may one day say of us, "How great is your love!" (**Luke 7:47**).

5

Princess Tamar

SUFFERING OF THE RIGHTEOUS

(II SAMUEL 13)

Princess Tamar - The daughter of King David, the sister of Absalom. She has grace and nobility. She is so beautiful that men feel sick with love just to see her walk by. Even the crown princes are crazy about her.

Amnon is David's first born son but through a different wife from Tamar's mother. Amnon is one of those who are "sick" in love with her. He, like all the rest of the young men in the country, just can't get her out of his mind. He fantasizes about being with her. His romantic love turns to lustful imaginations. He must have her. He wants to get his hands on her but does not know how.

His friend Jonadav discovers Amnon's secret fantasies. He sets up Tamar. Tamar comes to serve Amnon having been told that he is sick. She is sweet and servant-like, happy to be of help. Yet the minute they are alone, Amnon forces her and rapes her, despite her pleadings for him not to do it. Then in his violent perversion, Amnon throws her out of the house after having raped her.

This young girl, who was on the top of the world just a brief moment ago, has had her life ruined. She is distraught, almost insane. She tears her clothes and throws dust upon her head. But it is too late; it is all over.

Her brother Absalom fumes with anger. He seeks revenge, and two years later he has Amnon murdered. But what about Tamar? She is told just to shut up. There is nothing to do. There is nothing that can restore her to her idyllic position. She has lost her virginity and lost her posture as princess. She has been used and abused.

In the world that is dominated by evil men and in which women are just objects for their pleasure, Tamar is now simply soiled and spoiled merchandise. This is the last we hear of her in the Bible. The injustice of this situation is unbearable and unthinkable.

I wonder how many women can relate to her story. They were sweet and beautiful, and the world abused them brutally. They wanted to serve the Lord, and all they got was destruction and pain at the hands of evil men. What about the Christian teenage girls in Nigeria who were kidnapped and raped by the Boku Harum? Or the Kurdish teenage girls raped by ISIS? Or young women in Jewish, Christian or secular homes who are abused by family members, neighbors, employers, educators—or, God forbid, even pastors, priests or rabbis? There are no answers. It is despicable.

[Of course, such evil demands judgment from God. And those who perpetrate such crimes will suffer punishment. So there are answers eternally. Ultimately, there is perfect justice. But in the immediate set of circumstances, sometimes there are no apparent solutions.]

In an unrighteous world, the innocent suffer. The world forgets about them. But God does not forget. For this reason I think Tamar's story is in the Bible: just to tell us that God will not forget her. It is recorded officially. Perhaps you have been brutally mistreated, and there is nothing anyone can do about it. No one can even know what you have gone through. This is true of men just as it is of women. There are millions of others like you. Tamar's story is in the Bible for you.

This is also one of the reasons that Yeshua was crucified. He was an innocent lamb brought to the slaughter. He was stripped, mocked, beaten and spit upon, even though He had done no evil. He took the sins that evil people have done to innocent people upon Himself. That is how He made atonement for us. Only in Him can we find solace and redemption. **By His stripes, we are healed – Isaiah 53:5.**

Righteous people in an evil world suffer. **Through great tribulation we must enter the kingdom of God – Acts 14:22.**

Everyone who wishes to live righteously in Messiah Yeshua will be persecuted – II Timothy 3:12. We do not have a choice of whether we will suffer; we do have a choice as how we will react to it. The first thing to know is that God sees, knows, remembers and writes everything down in His Book. The story is not finished.

Both Amnon and Absalom are in danger of horrible and perhaps eternal punishment on Judgment Day. Listen to the logic of how judgment was described to the abusive and wealthy man who was assigned to punishment in hell while the poor abused beggar at his gates (Lazarus) received eternal reward in paradise: **Luke 16:25 – "My son, remember that you received your good things in your lifetime, while Lazarus received bad things. Now he is comforted while you are tormented."**

What fear of God that thought gives! Our perspective on eternal life and justice puts present suffering in a different perspective altogether. **"The sufferings of this present world are not worthy even to be compared to the glory which will be revealed to us" (Romans 8:18).** Perhaps Tamar will receive glory for eternity. A million years from today, her suffering will just serve as an example of and a testimony to the grace of God. Yet during her lifetime that experience was real and disastrous.

As we turn to God in times of suffering, there is a special comfort of the Holy Spirit (**I Peter 4:14**). The Holy Spirit is the Comforter (**John 14:16; 16:7**). And through the anointing of the Holy Spirit we can receive healing on the inside. God's love can **"heal the broken hearted... comfort all who mourn... give them beauty for ashes, the oil of joy for mourning, the** garment of praise for the spirit of heaviness" (Isaiah 61:1-3). God can turn our mourning into joy (John 16:20-22). This deep source of inner encouragement does not necessarily change the outward circumstances, but it can give us the patience and strength to bear it.

Many people are broken hearted. God takes special notice of those who have been through heart-breaking situations. He is particularly "near to those who have a broken heart" – Psalm 34:18.

It is not just that God is near to them, but He receives their suffering as an "offering" unto Him. "The sacrifices of God are a broken spirit; a broken and contrite heart, O God, You will not despise" – Psalm 51:17. Even if nothing seems to work out in this world, God receives you and loves you. He receives your suffering as an act of worship unto Him. And that worship begins to turns the situation to good.

And not only that: God will not leave you with a broken heart. He will heal you. "He heals the broken hearted and binds up their wounds" – Psalm 147:3. The suffering is temporary; it will not last forever. You will be healed as you turn to God's grace. The world wounds and God heals.

We can trust that something good will yet come out of the situation. For all Jacob knew, his beloved son Joseph had been dead for thirty years. He had not had one single day of happiness in over three decades. All his dreams were shattered. It was a situation that could not be repaired. Jacob had decided just to wait for his own death in the midst of depression and hopelessness. But in the end, it turned out that Joseph had become the savior and ruler of Egypt, and Jacob's dreams came true.

Romans 8:28 - We know that God causes all things (even the bad things) **to work together for the good for those** (us) **who love Him and are called according to His purposes.**

Nonetheless, the suffering of innocent people is a very difficult and painful subject. It is heart-breaking. Yet in all the biblical descriptions of the righteous suffering, there emerges one last profound secret: *Standing in faith through trials and tribulations produces godly character.* As gold is refined in fire, so is godly character refined through difficult experiences.

I Peter 1:6-7 – You are joyful even if it is necessary for you to suffer for a time in all kinds of trials in order that your faith, refined and precious much more than gold… will come forth into praise, glory and honor.

Peter went on to say that times of suffering are like a fiery ordeal, and it seems so bad that it is outright bizarre (**I Peter 4:12**). Yet, the fire will end; the gold will remain. You will come out of this situation shining like gold. And that gold is beautiful and precious.

Standing in faith through trials and tribulations produces godly character. How can that be? Here is what James said:

James 1:2-3 – Consider it great joy, my brothers, when you come into all kinds of trials, for you know that the testing of your faith produces patience.

And Paul agreed with both Peter and James:

Romans 5:3-4 – We glory in tribulations, knowing that tribulation produces perseverance; and perseverance, character; and character, hope.

God created us in His image. He desires to develop godly character within us. Godly character results in us being glorified together with Him. Even Yeshua had to suffer before being glorified. To the degree that we suffer with Him, we will also be glorified with Him. This is a difficult concept to grasp: Godly suffering produces character, and to the degree that we suffer for righteousness in this life, we will be glorified in the world to come.

There is nothing essentially good about suffering. God does not want you to suffer. He is not sadistic. When God created the world, before sin in the Garden of Eden, there was no suffering (**Genesis 2**). In the fulfillment of the plan of God, when sin and its effects are removed, there will be no suffering for the rest of eternity (**Revelation 21**).

Character is not developed by suffering *per se* but by being faithful and obedient in the midst of suffering. Suffering does not produce character; it is the faithfulness through the times of suffering that produces character.

Faithfulness is faith that has passed the test of time. Faithfulness is faith that has come through difficulty. If there is no difficulty, there can be no opportunity to develop faithfulness. As in athletic training, proper conditioning can only be developed by pushing through resistance.

It is not the suffering that is sought after but the obedience, faithfulness, generosity, humility, patience, love and purity in the midst of suffering that is so precious. Your godly and Christ-like character is a pearl of great price; it is beautiful in the eyes of God. Even Yeshua Himself had to go through a process of being "perfected" by obeying in the midst of suffering (**Hebrews 5:8; Philippians 2:8**).

I want you to have that godly character. I want you to have that precious jewel within you. I want you to receive all of your glory in the world to come. I want you to be encouraged and strengthened in the midst of your suffering in this life.

Part of the mystery is that suffering and glory go together. Not only do they go together, but suffering and glory come in equal measures. To the degree that we suffer with Yeshua, we will also be glorified with Him.

Romans 8:17 – Indeed if we suffer with Him that we may also be glorified together.

The connection between suffering and glory is profound. Yeshua suffered and then was glorified. By His sufferings, He shares in your sufferings. By your suffering, you share in His. There is a place of intimate fellowship with the Lord in times of pain and difficulty. In fact, there is a depth of intimacy which can only be experienced in times of suffering.

Philippians 3:10 - ... that I might know Him in the fellowship of His sufferings.

I believe that in the world to come, Princess Tamar will be restored to her place of royalty and beauty. And for those of you who have gone through needless and senseless suffering and abuse, for no fault of your own, you too will be restored to a place of glory and destiny.

6
Miriam of Bethany
POURING OUT EXPENSIVE WORSHIP
(MATTHEW 26:6-13, MARK 14:3-9, JOHN 12:1-8)

Let's look now at Miriam (Mary) of Bethany, a woman who expressed her worship to God in a most precious and extravagant way. She poured out her soul and spirit, as well as expensive perfume, in devotion to Yeshua.

(**Note**: *Some people see this event as the same as the sinful woman in Luke 7. However, the type of worship is different in the two events. In any case I have related to the two in different chapters because of the different lessons learned.*)

There was a brother and two sisters – Lazarus, Martha and Miriam – who were among Yeshua's best friends. They lived in a small village on the east side of Jerusalem, called Bethany (Bet Aniah, House of the Needy, בית ענייה in Hebrew or today called by the Arabs, *El Azariah,* presumably from the name Lazarus).

Everyone knew that these were Yeshua's close friends. When Lazarus died, before Yeshua raised him from the dead, the people wondered why Yeshua had not tried to save such a close friend whom He loved.

Martha and Miriam were close women friends. This is the Martha whom Yeshua encouraged not to be upset by so much workload and responsibilities that she would miss the "best part" of being close to Him (**Luke 10:41-42**). But her sister Miriam certainly did not miss that part of being close to Yeshua. Maybe Martha was getting frustrated that Miriam was not helping out with the chores like she should, but to miss personal time with Yeshua? – forget it!

Perhaps Miriam was a little spoiled, a little self-centered, a little pampered; or maybe just seemed that way to her sister. We do not know. But she did have a passionate love for Yeshua that embraced all of her being, her emotions and her thoughts – all of who she was as a human being and as a woman. When her brother died and Yeshua had not come to heal him, she seems to have taken it personally, a little too personally. It was as if her feminine pride had been offended.

When Yeshua came to Bethany after Lazarus died, it was Martha the responsible one, of course, who came to greet Him. It was her amazing faith that said to Yeshua that she believed that even after her brother's death, Yeshua could raise him from the dead. **John 11:21-22 – Martha said to Yeshua, "Lord, if you had been here, my brother would not have died; but even now I know that anything you ask from God, God will give you."**

Wow! Although her faith was not totally clear at that point, she believed in Yeshua, in the resurrection, in supernatural healing and in the unlimited power of prayer in an extraordinary way. "Even now," she said, "I know." (Perhaps it was because of her faith that God delayed Yeshua's coming to the tomb for four days.)

For whatever emotions Miriam was feeling at the time, she did not come.

However, when she heard that Yeshua was calling for her, she leaped up and ran to Him (**verse 29**). She fell at His feet and began to weep. When Yeshua saw her weeping, He was shaken and stunned. **John 11:33 – When Yeshua saw her weeping, and the Jews who came with her weeping, He groaned in the spirit and was shaken.** When she wept, then He wept. It is in immediate reaction to her weeping that Yeshua asked to know where the tomb was and headed in that direction to raise Lazarus from the dead (**John 11:34-36**).

The emotional reaction of Miriam and Yeshua to one another was powerful.

When Judas Iscariot saw Miriam pour out expensive oil on Yeshua, Judas decided to betray Him. Judas was offended. Part of his offense was certainly greed, because of his stealing money from the ministry team's purse. Another part was a prideful reaction to Yeshua's claims of lordship and divinity. However, it seems to me from the texts that there was also a bit of jealousy at the intensity and intimacy of the relationship between Miriam and Yeshua (**Matthew 26:7-13, Mark 14:3-9, John 12:3-5**). It can not be a coincidence that Judas made his final decision to betray Yeshua right after he saw Miriam anoint Him (Matthew 26:14; Mark 14:10; John 12:4).

[**Note:** Several popular novels have proposed a scenario in which Yeshua had a scandalous romantic and sexual relationship with Mary Magdalene. That makes no sense. If there had been a relationship, there would be no reason to hide it. They could have gotten married. All of Yeshua's disciples had wives. Most of the great prophets of Israel were married. There would not necessarily have been a problem from a Jewish social and religious point of view for the Messiah to be married.

In addition, we do not see the close personal relationship with Mary Magdalene as we do with Mary of Bethany. If someone wanted to make up a fantasy about a romantic relationship with Yeshua, it would have been Mary of Bethany and not Mary Magdalene.]

There was something obviously very passionate and personal in the way in which Miriam worshiped Yeshua that made everyone else feel irritated. I am not saying that they had a romantic relationship and certainly not any improper sensual relationship. However, the way in which Miriam "poured herself out" for Yeshua included all of her being and emotions, including her identity as a woman. There was a feminine and intimately passionate aspect to her devotion to Him.

The **Song of Solomon** compares the love of Israel and God to the love between a husband and wife. The spiritual worship between God and His people is compared to sexual and marital love. The "bridal paradigm" includes all of us who worship God, men and women, Jew and Gentile. We who love God are all part of His "bride." It seems that the heart of Miriam of Bethany was filled with the passion of the **Song of Solomon** in her attitude toward Yeshua. Miriam was like a personal embodiment of the **Song of Solomon**. And Yeshua certainly seemed to want to protect her feelings for Him.

When the disciples ridiculed Miriam for her worship passion, He rebuked them all and commanded them to tell her story to the whole world. **Matthew 26:13 – Truly, I say to you, that in every place where this gospel will be proclaimed, in all the world, it will be told also what she has done, and that as a remembrance to her.** His rebuke apparently motivated them rather strongly.

From Yeshua's point of view, it did not matter if Martha became irritated, if Judas betrayed, if the disciples protested or if the poor had to wait. They all got the message: "don't mess with Miriam, particularly when she is worshiping Yeshua."

Sometimes I see my wife praying or worshiping in a way so intimate and so deep that it seems to be painful. If I even come close to interrupt her intimacy with the Lord, I can feel the sweet and jealous anger of the Lord. "You may be her husband, but don't even think about interrupting her intimacy with Me." All I can think on the inside is, "Yes, Sir."

I have heard more than one testimony about men who were jealous of their wife's intimacy with the Lord during worship times.

John 12:3 – Then Miriam took expensive and pure alabaster perfume, three hundred grams in weight, and anointed the feet of Yeshua and wiped them with her hair, and the house was filled with the fragrance of the perfume.

Mark 14:3 – Then came a woman holding a bottle of alabaster oil, pure and very expensive. She broke open the bottle and poured out the alabaster on His head.

It is interesting that the gospel writers took note of the fact that the perfume was very expensive (men, I guess!?). So it must really have been unusually expensive. But Miriam saw it as an expression of her worship and love. It was like a man buying an expensive ring for his fiancée. There is no price to express the love. Miriam's passion was priceless to her and, therefore, priceless also to Yeshua.

I am thankful to Mike Bickle and all of our friends at International House of Prayer Kansas City who have restored the vision of extravagant worship to the Lord. The issue is not money (anyone who has been to IHOPKC knows that they all live in a very modest, even austere style). The issue is worth.

Price is in the eyes of the beholder and not in the budget. They put their best into worship – their best time, their best energy, their best skills and talents. Our dear friend Rose, one of the founders at IHOPKC, is another example of a young woman "pouring herself out" in worship and devotion to Yeshua.

To worship God is to show Him that you love Him. Loving God is the greatest commandment (**Deuteronomy 6:5; Mark 12:30**). Mike teaches that we should put the first commandment as the first priority in our lives.

My friend Paul Wilbur is also that way. He wants all the technical aspects of worship, sound, instruments, recording and vocals to be top quality. If it is expensive, so be it. It is not just an issue of artistic pride but a desire in his words, to "make His worship glorious." Worship must be excellent and expensive if it is to be glorious. (Again, the issue is not the money but the devotion.) There is a desire to make worship top quality and the top priority of our lives.

We feel the same way at Revive Israel. We have our whole team invest two hours every work day to worship before the Lord first thing in the morning. This kind of priority in time, staff and energy to be poured out on Yeshua is quite expensive in materials, salaries and budgeting. (Although we cut operating expenses to the bare minimum, and our buildings and offices are located in an old industrial zone.)

The overall investment in "prayer, praise and prophecy" is overridden by our passion to worship Him. During our morning times, we seek to listen to His voice, to produce local worship sounds in Israel, and to prophesy from the revealed Word in Hebrew. Everyone on our team knows that this is the source of spiritual inspiration for everything else we do.

We desire not only to pour out the best oil on the Lord every day, but to "produce" or "buy" that anointing oil by our dedication, sacrifice, passion and worship. We do not want to be like the foolish virgins who did not take the time to purchase the oil for their lamps (**Matthew 25:1-10**).

As we look to the book of **Revelation,** we see that there is ongoing worship in heaven. In the end times, the saints are to connect their worship on earth to the worship that is going on in heaven. This connection in "two-level" worship opens the heavens above us and releases the power of God from heaven into earth (**Revelation chapters 4, 5, 8, 11, 15**).

In fact there is a "war" over worship. In the end times, the devil and the anti-Christ will force everyone to worship them (**Revelation 13:4, 8**). The "Beast" government will attack everyone who tries to worship God (**verse 7**). This war over worship will be a matter of life and death (**verse 8**). However, the true worship by the saints in the end times will overcome the power of the Beast (**Revelation 15:2-4**).

At Revive Israel we dare to believe that we are involved in "Book of Revelation style" prophetic worship on a day to day basis. We desire to be connected to the worship that is going on at the same time in heaven. Of course that connection could be hundreds of times stronger, but the purpose in our hearts to start each day with that heaven-to-earth harmony is the highest priority.

Let us be a worldwide company of Miriams, pouring out our hearts unto the Lord with expensive worship and priceless passion. This applies to both men and women. We are all the "bride" of Christ. Let Yeshua feel our passionate dedication and love for Him. And may this release a new dimension of prophetic anointing and perfume in these end times!

7

The Poor Widow

SEEDS OF SUPERNATURAL GENEROSITY

(LUKE 20:45-21:4)

When Yeshua and His disciples made their final entrance into Jerusalem before His death and resurrection, they were walking by the Temple near the place where people would donate financial offerings to the work of the priests. There He saw wealthy people coming to make large donations, many of whom were making a show of how much they gave.

He emphasized that when one gives money, it must be for pure motives. Developing right motives for generous giving was a main subject that Yeshua dealt with in the Sermon on the Mount. **Matthew 6:1 - Take heed that you do not do your charitable**

deeds before men, to be seen by them. Otherwise you have no reward from your Father in heaven.

In addition to the wealthy making a show of their giving, there were also religious leaders, members of the Levitical priesthood at that time, who were motivated more by greed than by true devotion. Unfortunately, today there are many people in different kinds of ministries and charity organizations who manipulate people to give. Their motives and their methods are often not pure.

Recently, I was sharing with a small group of younger disciples. I realized that some of them had been offended about fundraising issues, particularly concerning Christian support for Israel and Messianic Jews. As we chatted, I told them, "I'm sorry to say this but in the majority of cases, motives and methods of fundraising are not totally pure. You must set your mind to make two quality decisions: First, do not let others' incorrect actions make you stumble; second, determine that you will always act with integrity and generosity yourself, no matter what the cost."

We must always make sure that what we think we are doing "for God" or "serving His Kingdom" is not just an excuse to raise funds. To "make merchandise" of spiritual things is a grave and widespread sin. Let us choose to walk in sincerity and integrity despite what many others may seem to do. **II Corinthians 2:17 – For we are not, as so many, peddling the word of God; but out of sincerity… speak in the sight of God.**

As Yeshua finished rebuking both the wealthy businessmen and the religious leaders for their hypocrisy (**Luke 20:45-Luke 21:1**), He also noticed a poor widow who came and gave two coins of small worth. He remarked, **"This poor widow has given more than them all, because all the others gave offerings out of what they did not need, but she from out of her lack has given all that she has to live on" – Luke 21:3-4.** The timing of His rebuke of the hypocritical leaders and the commendation of the poor widow, one right after the other, gives us a clear contrast between two types of attitudes in giving.

The woman did not give more quantitatively than the others, but she did give more qualitatively. It is as if God's accounting and arithmetic works not by total sum but by percentage. Even if the most generous of the wealthy gave huge amounts totaling up to 50 percent of their resources, it could not compare to this woman who gave 100 percent. We should be inspired by the fear of God to be aware of the fact that God takes notice of what we give, why we give and how much we give.

When Yeshua said that the poor widow gave more, He was referring to her faith. Obviously, it takes much more faith to give what you need to live on than to give what you can spare. She had no money in savings and had no husband to support her.

In speaking of women and giving, it is significant that it was primarily a small group of women who supported Yeshua's ministry financially. These women accompanied Yeshua alongside the twelve "apostles." **Luke 8:1-3 – He went through every city and village, preaching and proclaiming the good news of the kingdom of God. And the twelve were with Him, and certain**

**women who had been healed of evil spirits and sicknesses –
Mary… Joanna… Susanna, and many others who provided
for Him from their possessions.**

Part of the band of traveling disciples that accompanied Yeshua
was this group of women. Yeshua had women disciples as well as
men. In fact there were "many others" of them as well. In our
teams, there are always spiritual "daughters" that serve with us,
along with the spiritual "sons." The women on Yeshua's "team"
had a heart of generosity. The support of these women provided
the primary financial base for Yeshua's ministry. They were an
integral part of His team (**Galatians 5:22**).

Generosity is one of the most basic characteristics that God
wants to develop in us. It is one of the fruits and gifts of the
Spirit (**Romans 12:8, II Corinthians 8:7**). Yeshua taught that
giving is as important of a spiritual discipline as prayer (**Matthew
6:1-6**). We want to be "aggressively" generous givers. As we seek
to develop the godly characteristic of giving, the example of the
"poor widow" who gave all she had helps to set the standard of
generosity, sincerity and integrity.

We believe that the best way to give is to set percentage guidelines
from the beginning before the flow of money starts to come in
or go out. The percentage guidelines should be set according to
spiritual goals. We tell congregations and ministries connected
with us that a good pattern is to set aside in the budget one-third
of the general donations received. Many people think that they
would like to give. They believe that as soon as their congregation
or ministry organization has enough money, they will give. But

that is a misconception. As the income gets larger, so do the costs and expenses. The same holds true for personal finances.

Giving is best done in two separate actions:

1. Setting the budgeted money aside.

2. Giving the money out.

It takes too much faith to do both actions at the same time. There is wisdom to determine how much to give and in what direction. There is faith to determine where and to whom to give it.

Staff members involved with processing the giving out of charitable funds should not be involved in the decision-making process to determine whom to give to. That would put the staff member in a position to be manipulated by people requesting money.

We do not want to be led in our giving only by the immediate circumstances and chronic needs. Rather, we want to set guidelines ahead of time in order to be able to give more strategically and more generously. Setting money aside first according to a percentage-based plan increases both the amount we will actually be able to give and the wisdom of how to give it.

Giving is a fundamental value and should be done with a strategy that matches the overall Kingdom vision and purpose of the organization, congregation or family. When Paul (Saul) started his new apostolic ministry to the Gentile world, the apostles in

Jerusalem asked of him just one thing: to remember the poor and needy (**Acts 11:29, Romans 15:27, Galatians 2:10**).

Giving is such a core heart issue that it is part of the very definition of love and of the gospel. **God so loved the world that He gave His only Son... - John 3:16.** To receive money is a very temporary blessing, whereas, to give creates an eternal blessing. When we understand the potential of giving, it becomes much better to us than receiving. **It is more blessed to give than to receive – Acts 20:35.** Yeshua said that when we give to the needy, it is like a deposit in a heavenly bank, and we store up treasures for ourselves in heaven (**Store up for yourselves treasures in heaven - Matthew 6:20; Sell what you have and give to the poor; provide for yourselves... treasure in heaven that does not fail - Luke 12:33**).

The two great principles concerning finances are simply generosity and integrity. If we desire to be generous, our integrity will also be tested. Abraham provides a great example of integrity and generosity that was later blessed by God.

In one case, he yielded his personal rights for real estate in the Holy Land to his nephew Lot (**Genesis 13:9**). Immediately afterward, God blessed him with all the land his eyes could see (**Genesis 13:15**). In another incident, Abraham refused to compromise even on a "shoelace" when he could have received great wealth as spoils of war (**Genesis 14:23**). Immediately afterward, God blessed him with the great reward of the "Covenant of the Pieces" (**Genesis 15**).

And of course, there was Abraham's willingness to give up his "only son" Isaac on the altar, for which he was given the promise to be able to bless "all the nations of the earth" (**Genesis 22:2, 18**). What Abraham gave up as seed was multiplied millions of times. The testing of integrity comes before the blessing of prosperity. We give of a little by faith, and then God allows for us to give much more.

There will be a need for supernatural faith giving in the end times. The Bible tells us that the world economic system will turn evil (**Revelation 13:16-17**) for a period of seven years. Yet in the time of Joseph in Egypt, the financial difficulty of seven years turned out to be a great blessing for the Kingdom. He responded to a dream in revelatory wisdom and changed the world. In fact, he bought up all the money in the whole world (**Genesis 41**).

God created all the gold as good (**Genesis 2:10**). Joseph bought all the gold (**Genesis 47:14**). Moses took large portions of that gold out of Egypt at the Exodus (**Exodus 12:35-36**). This was all planned by God and promised to Abraham 400 years in advance (**Genesis 15:14**). That gold was used to build the Temple in Jerusalem. Solomon began receiving gold from all over the world (**I Kings 9:10-14; 10:2, 10-11, 14-25**).

There are also prophecies of the end times that **"the wealth of the nations will come unto you"** (**Isaiah 60:5, 11; 61:6; Zechariah 14:14**). While we do not know what all the circumstances are concerning this massive economic change, in all of them there may be seen references to Israel, to the Church and to the Messianic Jewish remnant.

Giving is not only in money but can be in spiritual things, such as prayer; it can be in practical ways, such as good works; it can be in training and sending people, such as students and children; it can be in words, such as teaching and witnessing. When we give, we plant a seed. Everything we sow will provide a harvest at some time (**Galatians 6:7-9**).

If we sow correctly, it will produce results of 30-fold, 60-fold and even 100-fold (**Matthew 13:8, Mark 4:8**). Moses went so far as to believe for a 1,000-fold blessing (**Deuteronomy 1:11**). And what of this poor widow herself? The example of her giving was written in the Bible, and countless people have been inspired to give because of her. Her one moment of total sacrificial giving has been multiplied throughout the generations countless times. How is that for producing results? I wonder what kind of treasure she has in heaven!

We should sow seeds every day and pray that those seeds would be blessed. Here are some examples of seed sowing:

- Giving to the poor

- Giving to congregations and evangelism

- Giving to works of social justice

- Doing good deeds

- Encouraging others

- Teaching in books and media

- Sharing the good news of salvation

- Serving others

- Spending time with others

- Raising children and grandchildren

- Raising students and disciples

- Prayers, praise and prophecy

Let us believe in the miracle that small seeds can increase miraculously. I try to pray often, if not daily, that the seeds of my life would multiply. When we look at the quantity of needs in the world, our ability to help seems insignificant. I feel like that poor widow. I would like to do much for the Kingdom of God, but what I have done seems so small that it seems almost meaningless.

But Yeshua said that even the small "gift" can be the biggest of all. Let us believe for supernatural multiplication of our seeds. It was also a poor widow, a single mother, to whom was given the miracle of multiplying the oil in the time of Elisha (**II Kings 4**). It was a young boy with a small lunch who ended up feeding thousands through the miracle of multiplication of the fish and the loaves at Yeshua's hands (**John 6:9**).

In all these cases, the point was the same: someone seemingly without means and with very little to give gave all that he or she had in great faith. That small seed of faith multiplied into great results. Isaac once planted seeds in the time of famine and God gave him a 100-fold return (**Genesis 26:12**). [An interesting note is that the word for 100-fold in this passage is "meah shearim" **מאה שערים** which was taken as the name for the famous ultra-Orthodox Jewish neighborhood in downtown Jerusalem today, which by a play on words also means "100 gates."]

I have seen a number of well-financed and well-publicized evangelistic events in Israel that produced much less fruit than what one might be made to think by the amount of publicity or quantity of the budget.

On the other hand, I know of one woman who helped take care of horribly crippled children in her home; and another woman, a single mother in financial difficulty, who began working with the needy. Both of these women ended up giving a significant testimony of faith that was broadcast on national television in Israel. Their "poor widow" type of giving of themselves and serving others was multiplied by faith much more than could have been imagined.

Perhaps what we have to give seems tiny to us; perhaps it is indeed tiny. Yet if we pray over all the areas of our lives and give what we have to give, then God can cause a multiplication that can change the world. Let us place ourselves in the same position as the poor widow that Yeshua saw at the Temple. Let us give of ourselves in faith and love. Let us know that whatever we sow in a right heart attitude will produce much fruit.

Give and it will be given to you, good measure, pressed down, shaken together, and overflowing will be given into your lap; for by the measure you measure out, it will be measured to you – Luke 6:38.

There will be a great return for giving, both spiritually and materially, both in this life and in the world to come. We do not know what happened in the story of the poor widow after she gave. We do know that her story was written in the Holy Scriptures for people in all generations to read. I suppose that is already an immeasurably great reward.

Let us be like that poor widow. Let us lower ourselves in extreme humility and poverty of spirit to be like her. In the midst of feeling that we have little or nothing to give, let us trust God that He sees what is in our hearts, and He can bless our little and turn it into much. Let us believe that supernatural generosity, multiplication and blessing will anoint all the different kinds of seeds in our lives.

8
Hannah
INTERCESSORY PRAYER
(LUKE 2:36-38)

In addition to Joseph, who was Yeshua's legal father, and Miriam, who gave birth to Yeshua physically, there is another "couple," a man and a woman whom I see as the "spiritual" parents of Yeshua. They labored in prayer to bring Him into the world.

They were both quite elderly, at the very end of their lives. They had spent decades interceding for the coming of the Messianic King. They were both prophets in their own right. The man's name was Simeon and the woman's was Hannah (Anna). They prayed and prayed according to the Messianic prophecies until the "word" literally "became flesh" through the birth of Yeshua. Their labor in intercessory prayer was what paved the way for Miriam to give birth in the natural.

I imagine that the wise men of the East (**Matthew 2:1**) had also been praying and interceding for decades and may be viewed as spiritual "uncles" to Yeshua. As Miriam, Joseph, Simeon, Hannah and the Wise Men were all involved in the process to bring about the first coming of Yeshua, so do I imagine that there will be different parts of Israel and the Church, both physical and natural, east and west, who will take part in bringing about the Second Coming.

This chapter is designed to prepare those whose hearts are called for intercessory prayer in the end times to "give birth" to the Second Coming of Yeshua and to His Kingdom on earth.

We can assume that the Wise Men from the East had become acquainted with prophecies about the Messiah from the teachings of the Jewish refugees and prophets who lived in Babylon and Persia at the time of the first great exile (586 BC). The teachings would have included those of Ezekiel, Daniel and Mordechai, among others. The "wise men" were not simply astrologers, but those who had studied the biblical promises and covenants, and understood that One would come as the King of the Jews to take up the throne of David.

Simeon was a righteous, religious Jew who lived in Jerusalem. The Holy Spirit came upon him and led him to go into the Temple (**Luke 2:25-27**). [Similarly, some of us as Messianic Jews have felt led by the Holy Spirit to enter back into our Jewish culture and religion as part of the expectation for the coming of Messiah.] In the Temple Simeon saw Joseph and Miriam who had come to offer the sacrifice to dedicate their son according to the priestly laws of the Torah (**Leviticus 5:11; 12:8**).

Simeon took the child in his arms, realized that this baby was the King Messiah he had been praying for all these years, and thanked God that he had finished his "mission" in life. Then Simeon blessed and prophesied over Miriam.

At the same moment, also led by the Holy Spirit, Hannah (Anna) entered the Temple and saw Miriam, Joseph and the baby. Hannah was of the tribe of Asher.

[**Note:** *This is a significant historical reference to the fact that the Jews kept the records of their family and tribal genealogies up until the destruction of the Second Temple. There were no "lost" tribes because they had these documents and were able to prove themselves to be members of all the tribes (including the northern ten tribes, like Asher). All those tribes were part of the Jewish community in Israel in the first century. This record keeping is also an affirmation of the validity of the documents of the genealogy of Yeshua as recorded in* **Matthew 1** *and* **Luke 3***.*

Since those types of records were destroyed in the destruction of Jerusalem in 70 AD, it would be impossible today for anyone to make a reasonably documented case for his being of the lineage of David today. This is yet another reason why no one else can claim to be messiah son of David today.]

Hannah was 84 years old, and had lived with her husband only 7 years before he died. The rest of those years (approximately 60) she spent in undivided devotion to prayer and intercession. **Luke 2:37 – She did not leave the Temple but served the Lord day and night with fasting and supplication.** Wow! This is undoubtedly a world record and even tops Moses' 80 days of prayer and fasting on Mount Sinai. She prayed tirelessly and unceasingly for 60 years. It took 9 months for Miriam's physical pregnancy, but it took 60 years for Hannah's spiritual pregnancy to give birth to the Messiah of Israel.

What focus, perseverance, dedication, purity, faith and revelatory understanding! I am sure there were many times during those 60 years of the conflicts with the Greeks and Romans before Yeshua's birth that she felt alone and overwhelmed. But she kept the faith, and she kept praying and fasting. She did not take a break at all. She lived through the Maccabees, the Essenes, the Sadducees, the Zealots and the murders of the Herod Antipater dynasty. These were birth pangs for 60 years and not just 60 minutes.

Unfortunately, the translation of Hannah's name to Anna breaks the obvious identification with another praying woman by the name of Hannah. She was the wife of Elkanah and the mother of Samuel the prophet. She could not bear a child. Because of this she began to intercede more deeply. She reached such a level of intensity in prayer that Eli the priest thought she was drunk (**I Samuel 1:13;** compare **Acts 2:13**).

Apparently God used the situation of her infertility to cause her to pray harder and harder. After extended intercessory prayer, she was able to give birth. The great prophet Samuel was born. He was the one who anointed David to become king (**I Samuel 16:13**), which in turn paved the way for the coming of the Messiah. So, unbeknownst to her, her distraught prayer had a part to play in bringing about the Kingdom of God and the birth of the Messiah.

Hannah's song of praise at the birth of Samuel, recorded in **I Samuel 2:1-10,** is surprisingly similar to Miriam's song of praise about the birth of Yeshua, as recorded in **Luke 1:46-55.** It is obvious that Miriam had read the prayer of Hannah often and identified with it in her heart. It is worth noting that the prayer of Hannah is part of the daily Morning Prayer in the Jewish Siddur prayer book.

Let us identify with Hannah's heart for intercession. Let us believe that God will raise up many spiritual daughters to Hannah of the tribe of Asher to pray whole-heartedly to overcome all the birth pangs and tribulations of the end times leading up to the Second Coming of Yeshua. There will be spiritual sons as well as spiritual daughters, all praying like Simeon and Hannah. As they prayed for His birth, we will pray for His return.

One of the keys to intercession is to believe that your prayers can really make a difference; that God will respond; that your words will come to pass; that angels will be deployed and demons bound.

In **Daniel chapters 9 and 10**, we find Daniel studying the Scriptures, repenting for the sins of the entire nation and asking for wisdom concerning Israel and the end times (**Daniel 10:14**). His prayers affected the spiritual warfare between the highest level of angels and demons and influenced the history of the Middle East and Europe for four to five hundred years to come.

In some of our times of intercession, we realized that we also had to repent for the sins of our people Israel and to repent for the sins of the Messianic Jewish remnant as well. The Lord showed us our racial and spiritual pride, how we have acted more like manipulative "Jacob" than noble "Israel." We have seen in prayer how our haughty attitudes have caused damage in our relations with the international Body of Messiah. During intercession on the model of Daniel's repentance for his people, we felt in our hearts and conscience the need to repent even of our own betrayal of Yeshua as a people.

At one point we shared this at a prayer meeting with leaders from the Chinese church, the Arab Christians, and internationals of many nations. The Holy Spirit broke through in the place, and there was deep weeping, repentance, intercession and reconciliation, including between the Jewish and Arab brothers. We had a sense that something historic was happening.

This repentance was continued later at the Homecoming 822 Conference in Jerusalem. With the International Convention Center filled to overflowing, some of us from across the Messianic body knelt on the convention stage and repented of our sins and pride. Impact from this intercession has been creating waves of intercession, touching parts of the Body all over the world, and in return, there has been a response of much greater commitment to Israel, to revival and to the Lord's return.

Yeshua taught that we have authority over demons (**Luke 9:1; 10:19**). He gave to us the keys of the Kingdom so that whatever we bind and loose on earth will be bound and loosed in heaven (**Matthew 16:19**). He also taught us that whatever we say in prayer will come to pass (**Mark 11:23-24**) and that whatever we ask in His name will be done for us (**John 16:23**). These are not only wonderful promises, they are powerful tools that we can use in intercession.

People ask whether we will be on earth during the tribulation, and if so how we will survive. The Bible teaches not only that we will be here, but that we will be victorious during that time. The seal of the Holy Spirit will protect us from harm (**Revelation 7:3**). Our worship will open the heavens (**Revelation 11:19; 15:5.** It seems to me these references are about people in heaven not earth). We will not be passive victims of the end times, but active agents, involved by faith in causing prophecies to come to pass.

Our prayers will rise before the Lord like incense (**Revelation 8:3**). Those prayers will be gathered over time like fire on the altar in heaven. When the time is right, angels will use the power of those prayers and throw them back down on the earth, and they will cause signs and wonders, earthquakes and thunders (**Revelation 8:4-5**). If we really understood the power of intercession, we would simply pray without ceasing.

In fact that is what Yeshua does with His time now and has been doing so for 2,000 years. **Romans 8:34 – He is found at the right hand of God and makes intercession for us.** Apparently He believes the most effective thing He can do is intercede for us. We should do the same. We can join Him in this labor of love.

Intercession is like any other prayer but deeper. Intercession means that there is such a deep identification with the people you are praying for that you feel you would be willing to give your life for them (**Romans 9:3**). In intercession your desire for the prayer to be answered goes deeper than words can express and comes out like groaning or in tongues (**Romans 8:26; I Corinthians 14:14**). There is an experience during intercession where you perceive that you are not just praying alone, but that the Spirit of God is praying together with you, for you and through you (**Romans 8:16, 26**).

While Yeshua was on earth, He also prayed often and for long periods of time. One night He spent all night in prayer for His disciples (**Luke 6:12**). That was almost one hour for each of them in one night alone. That's how a pastor should pray for his flock and a parent for his children.

Yeshua's habit was to rise every morning before dawn to pray by Himself in a field (**Mark 1:35**). (Don't forget that the sun rises very early in the Middle East and that He was often very busy until late at night.) It is amazing how much your life can change by developing a habit of early-morning prayer. Things will begin to change around you.

His prayers were passionate. He prayed with shouting, with weeping and with the fear of God. This is what it means to be a spiritual priest (and this kind of priesthood is open to man or woman, Jew or Gentile). **Hebrews 5:7 – In the days of being in a body of flesh and blood, He would offer up prayers and supplications, with great shouting and tears to the one who could save Him from death. Truly His prayers were heard because of the fear of God that was in Him.** To be a spiritual priest is to intercede like this on behalf of others.

Yeshua's prayers were offered up like temple sacrifices. Why did He weep? Because He felt the pains of those He was praying for in deep compassion. Why did He shout? Because He was fighting against opposition and pushing back the forces of evil in the world. Why did He have the fear of God? Because He knew God is Holy and hates evil (**Proverbs 8:13**).

So much can be accomplished in prayer. Here are a few things you can do:

1. Dedicate your daily schedule to the Lord (**Psalm 31:15**)

2. Pray for others to have wisdom and revelation (**Ephesians 1:17**)

3. Pray for Israel to be saved (**Romans 10:1**)

4. Pray for success in all you do (**Joshua 1:8; Psalm 1:3**)

5. Thank God for all His grace to you (**Psalm 136; Philippians 4:6**)

6. Ask for the Lord's will to be done in your life (**Matthew 6:10; 16:24; 26:39**)

7. Forgive others (**Matthew 6:12; Mark 11:25**)

8. Ask God to forgive your wrongdoings (**Matthew 6:12; Mark 11:25**)

9. Change the elections (**Daniel 2:21, 4:17**)

10. Give direction to government leaders (**I Timothy 2:2**)

11. Move angels (**Hebrews 1:14; Daniel 10:12-13**)

12. Dedicate yourself to holiness (**Numbers 15:39; I Thessalonians 4:3**)

13. Know that God likes you (**Luke 3:22**)

14. Bind demons (**Luke 10:19**)

15. Divide demons (**Luke 11:17**)

16. Receive financial, material and spiritual provision (**Matthew 6:11**)

17. Receive wisdom to know what to do (**James 1:5**)

18. Bless your children (**Psalm 127:4; 128:3**)

19. Bring unity to the Church (**John 17:21-23**)

20. Bring unity within Israel and between Israel and the Church (**Ezekiel 37:16-17, Romans 11:17**)

21. Invite Yeshua to return (**Matthew 23:39, Revelation 22:20**)

And the list goes on and on and on...

Really there is no end to what can happen through prayer and intercession. It is the "engine room" and the "work shop" of the Kingdom of God. In the place of intercession, you can cause things to happen according to the will and purposes of God in your life and the lives of others.

Let us become intercessors like Hannah and Simeon, like Yeshua and the disciples, like Daniel and the prophets. Let us change the world through prayer, fasting, repentance and intercession. Let's be part of a company of "Hannahs" in these end times.

9

Yael
VICTORY IN
SPIRITUAL WARFARE
(JUDGES 4-5)

Many women today have risen to the highest positions in government. Golda Meir in Israel, Margaret Thatcher in England and Angela Merkel in Germany performed their duties as prime minister in a professional and worthy manner. There are also women who have taken major leadership roles in the "developing church" in many nations of the world, serving out of the need at hand and out of the calling of God, with a submissive, faithful and obedient heart.

We find another such example in the story of Deborah, leading the battle against the enemies of Israel. Deborah was both a prophetess and a judge in Israel (**Judges 4:4**), the judge being the highest place of government authority at the time. The same verse mentions her being married to a man named Lapidot. The implication here is that there was right order in her marriage, which gave affirmation of her position as prophetess and judge.

Canaanite forces under the leadership of General Sisera attack Israel. Deborah prophesies to Israelite General Barak that he is to lead the attack against the Canaanites. Barak says he will do it only if she accompanies him. He requests her leadership. She agrees to go but rebukes him saying that since he was fearful to lead the battle alone, the commander of the enemy army, Sisera, will be given into the hands of a woman (**Judges 4:9**). The victory is won, but the order was less than perfect (although perhaps even more humiliating for the enemies of Israel at the time).

That woman turned out not to be Deborah but Yael (Jael), the wife of Heber, an ally of Israel. Sisera flees from the battlefield. Yael meets him and invites him to take refuge in her tent. When he falls asleep, Yael stretches out her hand to the stake of the tent, approaches him quietly, and then hammers the tent peg into the side of his head, thus killing him instantly. (The scene would have been worthy of a Hollywood action movie.) The great evil warrior general falls at the feet of this Israelite young woman (**Judges 4:17-22**)

This true story serves as a parable for us today for the role of women in spiritual warfare. I very much identify with her as the image is applicable for men as well. But we can sense that Yael represents a special calling for women in these end times to destroy and "take down" evil rulers of demonic powers and principalities. As Yael won the battle for Israel, so today will women rise up in the image of Yael to fight the spiritual battles for Israel and the Church. They as well will "put their hand to the stake."

I think this is a sign that in the end times, some of the greatest spiritual battles will be won by women who fight the spiritual warfare from their tents, and not just by the famous men supposedly leading the battles. Spiritual warfare is an equal battleground for both men and women. The power and weapons that we have are spiritual and open to all in the name of Yeshua and the leading of the Holy Spirit (**II Corinthians 10:4-5**). We fight by the word of God as revealed in Scriptures and proclaimed with prophetic anointing (**Ephesians 6:17; Hebrews 4:12**).

Behind the evil events in our world are legions of fallen angels called demons. They are led by the chief evil angel, named Satan (**Revelation 12:7-9**). They are grouped together in ranks as in an army. There are major generals among those evil angels. They lead the demons in spiritual battles against the human race and against the saints of God. While they are strong in and of themselves as angels, they can be defeated by the word of God. Men and women alike can proclaim the word of God that tears down evil principalities.

The power of spiritual warfare is not in whether one is intelligent or wealthy; it does not matter if one is male or female, Black or White, Jew or Arab. It is determined by the faith of the person praying and proclaiming. The word of God when declared by faith in the mouth of a young girl or an elderly grandmother can defeat the greatest generals and rulers of evil principalities in the heavens above and around us.

I believe God is raising up an army to fight the spiritual warfare in these end times in the image of Yael. They will be an army of spiritual "Yaels." It will be an army of both men and women. One year at an international Aglow conference, Jane Hansen Hoyt and I called forth a stake to symbolize this spiritual battle. Someone had a metal stake in the auditorium and we brought it out on the stage with a hammer. Thousands took up this call to win the battles of spiritual warfare in our day.

The image of the stake is found not only in **Judges 4:21** but also in **Isaiah 22:23, Zechariah 10:4** and **Ezra 9:8.** In these passages the stake refers to:

1. The cross of Yeshua.

2. A weapon of warfare.

3. The restored remnant of Israel.

The spiritual battle of the end times as symbolized by the stake of Yael is connected to all three of these elements together.

Another image of women fighting spiritual warfare is the "daughter of Zion" shaking her head. **Isaiah 37:22 – "The virgin daughter of Zion has despised you. The daughter of Jerusalem has shaken her head after you."** What a powerful and poetic image this is. The princess-prophetess daughters of Zion merely shake their heads and wave their hair, and principalities of evil come tumbling down.

The shaking of the head is a universal sign of saying "No!" The waving of the hair is the woman's glory and spiritual power. She ridicules and rejects the forces of evil. Let the women today rise up as daughters of Zion and say "No!" to the powers of the world, the flesh and the devil.

This passage has even greater significance when we see it in context as an end times' prophecy. The armies of the nations come to attack Jerusalem; it is a day of tribulation (**Isaiah 37:3**). The head of the government of Israel turns to the prophets to ask for prayer support. Prayer is centered around the "remnant of Israel" (**Isaiah 37:4, 31-32**). Israel cries out, "Hosanna, Save us!" (**verse 20**) and at the last moment, the Angel YHVH intervenes and destroys the attacking enemies, and all Israel is saved (**verse 36**).

All the spiritual battles of the end times lead to one great apocalyptic war in which the nations of the world will attack Israel (**Ezekiel 38-39; Zechariah 12, 14; Isaiah 13**). At the focus of this attack will be an attempt by demonic legions to stop the restored remnant of Israel from inviting Yeshua to return to earth with cries of **"Blessed be He who comes in the name of YHVH"** (**Matthew 23:39**).

All spiritual attacks of satanic forces are ultimately intended to stop the Second Coming of Yeshua, and His Coming is integrally connected to the Messianic Jewish remnant in Israel. Therefore, evil spiritual attacks, whether directly or indirectly, are often connected to prevent that remnant from fulfilling its role in inviting Yeshua to return. End times' warfare is connected to the Second Coming of Yeshua, which in turn is connected to the Messianic remnant of Israel.

Therefore, a great spiritual victory is found as Israel and the Church are united in covenantal allegiance and cooperation. The Church should be Israel's natural and supernatural ally. They are connected by covenant through the God of Israel and the Messiah of Israel. It is easy to see the reverse in our generation as the demonic forces behind Islamic Jihad seek to kill both Jews and Christians. We should not be ignorant of these demonic plans (**II Corinthians 2:11**). What should be seen so obviously in the negative, we should see just as obviously in the positive.

As I write this chapter, there are terrorist groups surrounding Israel on all sides: Hamas in Gaza, Hezbollah in Lebanon, Boko Harum in Africa, and ISIS in Syria. Thank God that until this time He has protected our tiny nation. Yet much of this warfare is spiritual, beyond what is seen in the military and diplomatic fields. Israel cannot fight that battle alone. What Israel fights on the ground, the army of spiritual warriors must fight in prayer.

In order for there to be a united attack on Israel, there must be a worldwide, fanatic religion or philosophy to foment hatred against Israel. We see that today in the rise of anti-Semitism/anti-Zionism and of radical Islamic Jihad. There must also be some kind of international political organization that could unite the nations of the world before such an attack. We see such a world-wide organization today in the U N.

The hundreds of millions of Muslims in the surrounding countries outnumber Israel. The only way Israel can survive is for the Jihadic forces to be divided among themselves. The division among the Jihadists is a spiritual issue, as Yeshua taught in **Luke 11:17.** He said that if Satan's kingdom is divided amongst itself, it cannot stand. It is up to the interceding saints to prophesy a spiritual sword of division in order to keep the demonic forces behind the scenes divided, confused and attacking one another.

Many years ago I had a stirring experience in which I came to understand the strategic influence of proclaiming, **"The kingdom of Satan is divided, confused and fallen,"** according to **Luke 11:17.** I saw that by proclaiming this verse, a paralyzing and destructive power is released over demonic legions. I exhort you to take up this proclamation in faith as well. If we have authority to drive out one demon from one person, we also have authority to divide principalities of evil that are affecting millions. This prophetic prayer has exponential effectiveness.

Another spiritual experience that deeply affected me occurred at the Temple Mount in 1980. There I had a discernment of the evil powers surrounding Jerusalem, trying to prevent revival from taking place. These were mostly religious spirits, such as the ancient religious spirits in Islam, Christianity and Judaism. I realized that we (Israeli Messianic Jews) did not have enough power to overcome such strong principalities. I cried out in prayer for an answer. The answer I felt in my heart was that the revival would only come if true Christians were praying for us in every nation of the world.

There are some radical streams among ultra-Orthodox rabbinic Judaism that work hard to stop the movement of Messianic Jews in Israel. They try to lie to our people about us and about faith in Yeshua. This is why Yeshua rebuked the Pharisees in His day and called them spirits of serpents who prevent people from coming into the Kingdom of God.

It is interesting that Yeshua's rebuking of these evil religious spirits came in **Matthew 23** right before His statement that He would not return until the Jews in Jerusalem cry out **"Blessed is He who comes" (verse 39)** and His teaching on the end times in **Matthew 24.** The conflict with religious spirits in Israel in the first century serves as a foreshadow of the larger conflict facing us today in the twenty-first century.

The book of **Revelation** describes three major types of demonic strongholds: the Beast, the Dragon and the Harlot. In my understanding the Harlot is the spirit of decadence, corruption and sexual immorality coming primarily out of the West. The Dragon represents the insidious lies of the devil against the faith through false religious spirits and doctrines. The Beast represents violence, destruction and murder which we see today in the forces of Islamic Jihad.

Let us join together to become a spiritual army of love and truth that fights against these forces of evil by the word of God and the blood of Yeshua (**Revelation 12:10**). Let us stand in the image of Yael to win the spiritual battles of our day against all odds in the natural. May the international Church and the remnant of Israel rise together in prayer, praise and prophecy for victory in spiritual warfare!

10

The Woman with the Issue of Blood

PULLING ON THE POWER OF GOD
(MATTHEW 9:18-26, MARK 5:21-35, LUKE 8:43-48)

All of the women above in some way touched the heart of God by their faith, love and humility: in giving, in repentance, in prayer, in faith for her family, etc. However, if there is one woman above all who learned how to activate the power of God, it was an anonymous woman known throughout the world simply as "the woman with the issue of blood." Perhaps more than anyone else in history, she gave us the example of how literally to "pull out the power of God" by her faith.

We need here to make a distinction between the power of God and the Spirit of God. In the simplest description: the Spirit of God is a person, and the power of God is a thing. The Holy Spirit is Divine; the power is an energy created by God that can come through the Spirit. The power of the Spirit is often referred to as fire, but it can be likened to any kind of power.

[In Ezekiel chapter 1, the power of God is referred to in Hebrew by the word used today for electricity, Khashmal, חשמל. Throughout the writings of Luke, the Greek word for power is *dunamis*, similar to our words for "dynamic" or "dynamite."]

John the Baptist said that Yeshua would baptize us in the Spirit and in fire (power) – **Matthew 3:11.** Yeshua told His disciples that they needed to receive the Spirit and power. **You will receive power when the Holy Spirit comes upon you…** – Acts 1:8. That power came upon them in the form of fire, while the Spirit came upon them in the form of wind (**Acts 2:2-4**).

We react differently to the Holy Spirit from the way we react to the power. I liken the Holy Spirit to an electrical engineer and the power to electricity. We talk to the engineer; we use the power. The electrician and the electricity are related one to another, but they are essentially different in kind. One is a "who;" the other is a "what." We relate to the Holy Spirit personally in a way we do not to the power.

Towards the Holy Spirit, we are submitted. The Spirit leads us (**Romans 8:14**); we do not lead the Spirit. However, through the Holy Spirit, we are given power to use to do God's will. To submit to the Holy Spirit, we need humility. To use the power, we need boldness. To try to use spiritual power without submission to the

Holy Spirit is tantamount to witchcraft (**Acts 8:19-23**) and can even result in eternal punishment (**Matthew 7:21-23**).

Yet Yeshua told us that we must receive the power along with the Holy Spirit (**Acts 1:5, 8**). Walking in obedience, love and holiness always has priority over using the power, yet the power is also necessary in order to fulfill what He says.

Spiritual power, as with other forms of energy in physical nature, operates by certain laws and guidelines. The woman with the issue of blood demonstrated how to activate the power of God. She probably did not understand totally what she did or how she did it, but her example is more exact in detail than any other I can think of in Scriptures.

Yeshua was on His way to heal the daughter of Yair (Jair), the leader of a local synagogue. Crowds of people were surrounding Him, and everyone was bumping into one another. This woman had an unusual flow of menstrual blood for 18 years and had spent all her money on medical treatments to no avail. She pushed her way through the crowd in order to touch the hem of Yeshua's garment from behind.

Mark 5:28-30
For she said, "If I can even touch His garments, I will be healed."

In an instant the source of her bleeding was dried up and she felt in her body that she had been healed from her disease.

Immediately Yeshua perceived from within that power had gone forth from Himself.

Yeshua turns to the crowd and asks who touched Him. Considering the crowds all around them, His disciples think it is an unreasonable question. However, the woman knows she has been discovered. Of course in Jewish religious law, it is forbidden for a woman with a menstrual flow to touch any man, let alone an extended flow beyond the menstrual period, and even more unthinkable to touch the chief rabbi or the Messiah himself. From the point of view of her culture, she had committed an unforgiveable sin.

However, she came forward, fell at His feet, and told Him what had happened. Instead of rebuking her, Yeshua commended her saying, **"My daughter, your faith has healed you" – Mark 5:34.** Much has been taught on this passage by many teachers, so I will just summarize here briefly.

Yeshua was filled with power. She activated that power. Yeshua Himself did not decide to release the power, nor did He even know about it until the moment it happened. The healing came not because of His decision or His knowledge. It was all of her initiative. She did not ask His permission. She just "turned the power on." Or more properly, we should say, she "pulled the power out of Him."

There is no indication that there is something special about her. What she did could be done by any other person. Perhaps in the sovereignty of God, this incident happened with her because she would have been the most unlikely person to be considered a candidate worthy to activate the power of God. The very "lowness" of her social and religious position highlights the fact that the release of divine power is available to anyone and not dependent on the seemingly "worthiness" of the candidate.

The lesson we learn is that if she can do it, then anyone in the world can do it. The principle is universal like activating electricity. Receiving healing is like receiving forgiveness. If she could pull on the power of God, so could you and so could I. There is no favoritism here; there is just faith.

She had faith; she believed she would be healed. She did not doubt. She knew what she wanted. She was not looking for sympathy. She came to get healed. She got it.

She spoke words of faith. She "said" that she would be healed. As God created the world by words, so is the spiritual world activated by words today. She received what she said (**Mark 11:23**). In a house, one turns on the electricity by touching a switch or button. In faith, one activates the power by moving the tongue (**James 3:3-6**).

She made contact. Power is transferred by contact. Contact is not always by touch of hand; it can also be by simply hearing the word in the ear (**Luke 7:7**). Yet as an electric wire must make contact, so must faith make a connection in order for the energy to be transferred.

Yeshua felt the power going out of Him only at the moment it happened (**Mark 5:30**). That proves that it was not by His decision, His initiative or His effort. It all came from her. She also felt the power going into her at the moment that she was healed (**Mark 5:29**). They both felt the power but in slightly different ways. Yeshua felt the power go out of Him in His spirit; she felt the power go into her in her body.

It might be more correct to say she "felt" the power, while He "discerned" the power. In the Greek, what she did was ***gnosis*** and what He did was ***epignosis.*** As I understand this, *gnosis* means to "know" like "recognize". *Epi* means "inside" or "center" like "epicenter." So she knew and felt in the normal sense, but He knew and felt only on the inside of His spirit.

For spiritual *dunamis* power to go through us from God, it is not necessarily a "feeling" in the physical sense of the word, but it is more of an "inner knowing." The release of the power of God is not dependent on our feelings but on our inner connection with God in the spirit. This is important to know when ministering healing to others. Our ability to be a vessel of God's power can happen regardless of our emotional feelings; it is dependent more on that inner spiritual discernment.

This woman believed in Yeshua in some way as "Lord," a spiritual authority that she had to submit to in order to receive from God. She did not have an exact or well-developed theology. She just knew that He was the figure of authority she needed to submit to in order to be in right alignment with God. She knew that He was the connecting point for the power. She recognized that He had authority from God. She called Him Lord and fell at His feet as a sign of submission.

So those are the elements to release the power: faith, words, contact and submission to Yeshua. If the power could be released in this situation, so could it be in any other situation.

[**Comment:** *In all humility, it might be worth noting here that we do not always see the fullness of those miracles. Sometimes when Yeshua preached, everyone was healed (**Mark 6:56**); sometimes almost no one was healed (**Mark 6:5**). Concerning healing, there seem to be two general "modes" recorded in the New Covenant: one more "evangelistic," the other more "pastoral."*

The first kind is a confrontation of the powers of light and darkness when the gospel is shared publicly for all to see.

Mark 16:15-18 – Go into all the world and preach the gospel to all creation... They will lay hands on the sick and they will be healed.

To a certain degree, when an unbeliever sincerely listens to the gospel, he is beginning to repent in the sense that he is turning toward the Lord and away from whatever else he was doing at the time. There is an immediate opening for the power of God to be released. When the gospel is spread into new countries in a wave of evangelistic revival, supernatural healings are regularly experienced.

When ministering healing to members of a local congregation who are already believers, the Scriptures mention a second "mode" of healing, one with several more requirements.

James 5:14-16 – If there is any sick among you, call for the elders of the congregation and pray for him with the anointing of oil in the name of the Lord. And the prayer of faith will save the sick... And if he has sinned, he will be forgiven. Confess your sins to one another and pray one for another in order that you will be healed.

In this brief passage we see several factors which may hinder healing.

1. Broken relationships with others

2. Unconfessed sin

3. Unforgiveness

4. Lack of faith

5. Lack of submission to authority.

*There are many other factors as well: some having to do with the person receiving prayer and some having to do with those doing the praying. In many cases, it is not the fault of anyone involved, and often the reasons are just unknown (**John 9:1-3**). Most of the time, the causes are indirect and circumstantial. Let's not allow for cases in which people are not healed to discourage us. Doctors continue to work in the medical field even though not all are healed. So do we.]*

Yeshua Himself was filled with power. How did He get it? I believe the same way and by the same principles. He would arise every morning and go out early to pray with tears and shouting (**Mark 1:35; Hebrews 5:7**). As she received from Him, He previously had received in prayer from our Heavenly Father. As the woman got the power from Yeshua, so did Yeshua get the power from the Father.

If one can receive power to be healed, so can one receive power to heal others. What if this woman afterwards thought about what happened and said to herself, "If I received power for my own healing, perhaps I can receive power to heal others?"

What if she went out the next day early in the morning and began to "lay hold" of the power of God in prayer and faith? What if she then went out and proclaimed her testimony to others, and they began to come in large numbers to touch her and be healed by making contact by faith with the same power that she made contact with?

This woman's problem had not only been physical, it was social—she was an outcast. It was financial—she had spent all her money. It was psychological—what is wrong with me? It was religious —why am I an unclean woman? One moment of the release of the power of God solved all those problems. You can be healed in the same way in your emotions, memory, intellect, will and personality.

What if the woman with the issue of blood began to get hold of the power of God and release it in all kinds of other directions as well? She could pull on the power of God and pray for her family, for social justice, for successful businesses, for giving to the poor, for her community, for her government, for signs and wonders, for the salvation of Israel (**Romans 10:1**), for the unity of the Church (**John 17:21**), for the division and destruction of the kingdom of Satan (**Luke 11:17-18**), for the coming of Yeshua's Kingdom on earth (**Revelation 11:15**). Well, just about anything could happen.

The power of God through the Holy Spirit is unlimited. She did not wait for the Lord to decide. She took initiative to receive what God had already made available through Yeshua. Let's activate the power of God through faith and proclamation until the Kingdom of God comes to pass in fullness, and paradise is restored with heaven and earth joined together again (**Revelation 21-22**).

The version of the healing of the woman with the flow of blood in the gospel of Matthew gives a little insight into the Jewish-Hebraic background to the story.

Matthew 9:20 – A woman who had a flow of blood twelve years came up from behind and touched the hem of His garment.

Those with a knowledge of the Torah would immediately recognize the word "hem" as a possible reference to the "fringes" required on the hem of the garment (**Numbers 15:38, Deuteronomy 22:12**). The gospels do not say necessarily that she touched the fringes of Yeshua's garment, so we could interpret it either way as just the hem or the hem with the fringe on it.

Immediately after the woman was healed, Yeshua called her forward and made her "testify" of what happened to her. It occurs to me that many people in the crowd heard her story. Certainly they thought, "If that could happen to her, it could also happen to me." And that is exactly the response that Yeshua wanted.

Not only that, but they went out and began to tell their friends about the story until a multitude began to believe the same thing. Within a short amount of time, her faith had multiplied to many others. Just a few weeks or a few chapters later we read:

Matthew 14:35-36 – they brought to Him all the sick and requested from Him only to touch the hem of His garment, and all who touched were healed.

They obviously thought, "If she could touch His hem and be healed, why not me?" Not only did her faith spread to this multitude, but throughout history literally millions have read and been encouraged by her testimony in the gospels. She not only brought her own healing but healing to many.

This healing continues to multiply today and will continue into the end times. It will reach out to the nations around the world. Look how this miraculous "touching of the hem" comes into fulfillment in end-times prophecy.

Zechariah 8:22-23 – Many peoples and great nations will come to seek YHVH of armies in Jerusalem and to seek the face of YHVH… In those days, ten men from all the tongues of the nations will take hold and grasp the hem of a Jewish

man, saying, "Let us go with you for we have heard that God is with you."

In the fall of 2014, the International Convention Center in Jerusalem was filled to overflowing by the 822 Homecoming conference led by David Demian. The 822 referred to Zechariah 8:22. The majority of those in the conference were Christians from China. They came to worship in Jerusalem as a fulfillment of this verse and to fellowship with Messianic Jews and Arab Christians.

As we all prayed together, there was a powerful sense of spiritual healing flowing out to nations around the world: from Jews to Arabs to Chinese to virtually all the nations. Perhaps this was just a little taste of the ultimate **"healing of the nations"** that is promised in the end of days (**Revelation 22:2**).

God in His sovereignty allowed the woman with the issue of blood to reach a deep crisis in her life, a desperation, which led to an unusually profound and powerful faith. Let's stand with her to "touch the hem" of the Lord unto the healing of the nations. Let's make contact with the spiritual electricity and dynamite of God.

We must believe, pray and demand with that same desperate, tenacious and overcoming faith. Let us identify with this woman and how she pulled on the power of God through faith in Yeshua. Let us lay ahold of that same power of God until we see all of the promises and prophecies of God come true.

Let's be part of making it happen. There will be a worldwide army of women and men like her who will not let go of the power of God. Keep going! Keep holding on! What this woman started, we can finish.

11

Miriam of Migdal

KINGDOM BREAKTHROUGH

(JOHN 20:1-18)

On the shores of the Galilee, next to the village of Nahum (Capernaum), is another village by the name of Migdal. This village has become world famous because of a woman who grew up there, named Miriam, from whom Yeshua cast out seven demonic spirits (**Luke 8:2**). Miriam of Migdal is more popularly known as Mary Magdalene. She became one of Yeshua's most faithful disciples.

Miriam of Migdal may be best known for her coming to the tomb of Yeshua on the first day of the week after the crucifixion. She led several other women with her to the tomb before sunrise in order to anoint the body. However, when she arrived, the stone was rolled away, and the body was absent. The sequence of events is not exactly clear, but it seems that Miriam and her friends entered the tomb. There they were met by two angels that informed them that Yeshua had risen from the dead.

They ran back to tell the disciples. At first they did not believe the women, but then Peter decided to go check. Peter and John ran back to the tomb. John arrived first but waited outside. When Peter arrived, he went in. They saw the cloth that had been over Yeshua's face folded and placed on the side. John then says that he was the first to believe at that moment that Yeshua had indeed risen (**John 20:8**). Then the men returned home.

However, tenacious Miriam searched for the body (either before the men came or after they left). She thought perhaps the gardener had moved the body. At that moment, Yeshua came and stood behind her. She did not know who it was. Then He called her name, "Miriam." She recognized His voice and cried out, "Rabbi" (**John 20:16**). She then tried to hug Him, but He said, **"Do not touch Me for I have not yet risen to the Father"** (**John 20:17**).

By saying that He had not yet ascended, it seems that He had just been resurrected a short time before. What an astonishing moment this is! The Son of God has risen from the dead. The powers of darkness have been defeated. The universe has been changed from the "pre-resurrection-of-Yeshua" world into the "post-resurrection-of-Yeshua" world. And of all the people in history whom God could have chosen to be the first to see the risen Messiah, He chose Miriam. Miriam had the unique privilege of being the first person to see and try to grasp the risen Messiah.

Not only did Yeshua appear to Miriam first among all human beings after the resurrection, but He did so before He had even risen to appear before the Father in heaven. How could that be? He stopped the entire plan of world redemption in order to speak briefly with this woman? Yes. That was the influence of Miriam's faith on Yeshua. That was the level of Yeshua's commitment to her in return.

This was a breakthrough for the Kingdom of God of historic dimensions. So why did Yeshua choose to reveal Himself first to Miriam instead of the male disciples? I suppose the answer is simply that He was honoring her faith and the fact that she was the first to come to the tomb. Although Yeshua told her not to "lay hold" of Him physically, she was the one who did indeed lay hold of this paradigm shift in the Kingdom of God; she and not the great apostles. He sent her back to the disciples and they had to listen to what she said.

Afterwards, the disciples slowly realized what had happened and then took charge over the situation. Although she had the revelation first, the men stayed in position of authority. Should we ask the question then, why was she not appointed as the 12th apostle after Judas? Peter received authority when he had revelation about Yeshua being the Messiah (**Matthew 16:17-19**). Should not Miriam have received authority when she had the revelation about His resurrection?

This often seems to be the case, even today. The women are first to break through into a new revelation for the Kingdom of God. Then the men show up to take authority. Whether that is "unfair" is not the point. A question does arise as to what degree women are to hold positions of authority in the body of Messiah. Let's go back to the beginning:

Man and woman were called into a <u>partnership of dominion</u> over the earth (**Genesis 1:28**). God gave dominion over His creation to male and female together in unity. They are partners in dominion. The loving submission one to another on an equal basis, while maintaining the position of authority of the man at the same time, is what communicates harmony to the entire creation.

The children, the dogs and the cats, even the flowers and the trees, can all sense when mommy and daddy are hugging one another. The "dancing" harmony of husband and wife in love and authority releases blessing and order to all of creation.

In the created purposes of men and women, we also see a difference of tasks. The woman who gives birth is the primary source of life. (The name Eve in Hebrew is actually Chava חוות meaning, "life-giver" from the root of the word for "life" חי Chai.)

The man on the other hand is dedicated to working and to speaking. It was he who gave order to the animals by giving names to them. There is a connection here to the pattern that men have the primary responsibility for order, teaching and authority in the Church; this pattern is rooted in those first created functions of Adam and Eve.

Our desire is to encourage and release women into their spiritual calling, not to hold them back. The structure of authority is to protect and prosper them, not to restrict them. A man wants to extend his umbrella over his wife and children; not to subject them, but to protect them from the storm.

Yeshua was the greatest "liberator" of women in history, and the greatest example of loving and sacrificial male authority.

When Yeshua freed the woman who had been caught in adultery from being stoned (**John 8:1-10**), He established an important standard of equality of women before the Law. The Law should not be applied one-sidedly in order to oppress women. When we see how women are oppressed and abused in Muslim societies, "third world" nations, and even in some streams of Judaism and Christianity, we can appreciate just how much the New Covenant set a new standard for justice and honor for women. According to the New Covenant, women should have equal rights before any court of Law. Yeshua established equal judicial rights for women.

What might seem as a most abusive law of the Torah, in which a woman suspected of adultery is required to drink a mixture of water with dirt from a curse written in the ground before the altar (**Numbers 5:11-31**), was actually quite protective of her rights at that time. In a Middle Eastern honor culture, the man would have simply murdered her because of his feeling of jealousy. Here all he can do is make the priest give her a drink of dirty water. If nothing else happens, he is not allowed to harm her.

It would have required a supernatural intervention to prove her guilty. Without that supernatural intervention, the wife is assumed to be innocent. The Torah protected women from ancient Middle Eastern "honor killings." While the Law protected her from abuse, the gospel goes further to give her forgiveness altogether.

The presentation of the gospel provides the ultimate liberation for women. It is not the false liberation of Western humanism, which encourages sexual immorality, rebellion and occult spirits. Nor is it the suppression of women by religious legalism and coercion. The gospel is true liberation for women, first spiritually, then socially.

In this light, let us try to define what place or position a woman can hold in the congregation today. Two particularly challenging sections of Scripture are **I Corinthians 14:34-35** and **I Timothy 2:11-13,** in which Paul stated that women are not allowed to teach, or even speak, in the congregation (a practice which, by the way, is fairly well adhered to in ultra-Orthodox Jewish synagogues today).

The context of the Corinthian passages is the exercising of prophetic gifts in the congregational meeting. The purpose of the passage is to encourage the gifts, not to restrain them. We are told that **"everyone can prophesy" (verse 31),** but that we should have order and decency in the meeting (**verse 40**). The context seems to be not of limiting women from prophetic or teaching gifts but of maintaining order and authority in the assembly. In reading the entire chapter as a whole, one would note that the emphasis is on encouraging the gifts of the Spirit to all the members, including women, and not primarily on the restricting of women's involvement.

The Timothy passage is found right before the requirements for eldership in the congregation and, therefore, again seems to be an issue of authority. Understanding the restrictions on women speaking in the congregation as an issue of authority and order rather than the total prohibition of speech would seem to fit the context. In any case, because there are relatively few passages on the subject, there is room for a wider spectrum of interpretation and application.

We seek to find the balance between the openness of Holy Spirit inspiration to all of us equally as men and women, while maintaining the pattern of authority with men in senior leadership positions. How that comes into practice is different in different settings. It is even different between our congregation in Jerusalem and in Tel Aviv.

On a humorous side note: in our congregation in Tel Aviv, we have some older women from a Middle Eastern background who sometimes talk out loud in the middle of a teaching or prayer, and we have to lovingly encourage them not to interrupt ☺. We do not prohibit them from sharing in prayer or scripture, but we do ask them to refrain from disruptive talk during the meeting.

In the first century, there were three different cultures affecting the new congregations of faith in Yeshua: the Hebraic, the Greek and the Roman. The Greek culture was more oriented to freedom of women, whereas the Roman culture was more oriented to government authority. Hebraic and most Middle Eastern cultures were extremely conservative in the pattern of male and female roles.

In seeking balance in understanding the roles of men and women in a New Covenant community, the fundamental rule seems to have two parts, which may be summarized as:

1. ***Anointing*** *and ministry of the gifts of the Holy Spirit are open equally to men and women*

2. ***Authority*** *in the congregation is shared by men and women with men in positions of senior leadership*

Interestingly, women often receive inspiration and revelation of the Holy Spirit before the men (as in the case of Mary Magdelene or Lydia in **Acts 16:14**); and, women may take leadership authority when the men are not available or capable; or, when a special calling is recognized on the woman's life (as in the case of Deborah in **Judges 4**).

We do not see any place in the New Covenant where a woman has the office of an apostle or pastor. We do see, however, the daughters of Philip prophesying (**Acts 21:9**). That is certainly an example of speaking the word of God in the community of faith. Within the general pattern of men holding the positions of senior authority, the women are encouraged to minister whenever the Holy Spirit gives them a word for the community.

There may be an indirect reference to women evangelists as well in the Hebrew of **Psalm 68:11** which speaks of a great army of "hamevassrot" **המבשרות** – those who share the good news. In the passage, the word is in feminine form.

There seems to be a difference between the priestly calling and the prophetic. The prophetic is based on inspiration of the Holy Spirit and, by its very nature, is egalitarian. The priestly calling is to preserve the order of God's covenants. That's why we may have women operating in prophetic gifts, but we would not have a woman as a "priestess." The prophetic anointing is open to all; the priestly order preserves the role of men.

(When we speak of the "priesthood" of all believers, we are referring to a "prophetic" spiritual position, which is equal to men and women. That is not the same as a "priestess" position often found in occult religions.)

It is also worth noting that in the first century, the New Covenant was not written or available readily in book form. The oral teaching in the congregation was almost as authoritative as Scriptures. The community was submitted to observe the **"teaching of the apostles" – Acts 2:42.** Today in post-Reformation times, there is a deferring by all teachers, male or female, to the authority of the written text at hand.

In trying to maintain the right balance, we want to avoid the mistakes that can be made by extremism on either side. There are many congregations in which the spiritual gifts of women are suppressed; thus, the move of the Holy Spirit is also suppressed. There are other places in which the pattern of authority for the men is violated to the point that there is a negative influence on the order of God for the community, marriages and families.

If we all love and desire the full operation of the Holy Spirit, and also love and desire the order of God's authority, there should be little problem. Let's be careful not to lose that balance. Let's affirm the freedom of the inspiration of the Holy Spirit on one side and the structure of God's authority on the other.

Note that Phoebe is listed as a deaconess in **Romans 16:1.** All members of the congregation should serve within the congregation. A deacon is one who has proven himself trustworthy by taking responsibility for a significant area of service. If a woman has responsibility for that kind of area of service, then she is a deacon(ess).

If a man serves as an "elder," he is usually married. Therefore, his wife also has a role with him. The type of role she plays varies with the gifting and calling of the woman. Some prefer to be more active in public ministry, while others prefer a quieter, more private role. We should respect both kinds of marital partnership in ministry.

Man and woman in marriage are called to be partners in prayer and in ministry for the Kingdom of God. **I Peter 3:7 – You husbands should live together with your wives, knowing that the woman is the weaker vessel, and give them the honor as partners in the inheritance of the grace of life, in order that your prayers will not be hindered.**

I understand from this verse that men should treat their wives:

  1. With gentleness.

2. With honor.

3. As partners in the Kingdom.

4. As partners in prayer.

(This is parallel to the **Ephesians 5:25-33** passage in which a husband is called to "deliver himself" for his wife, be willing to die for her, glorify her, sanctify her, nurture her, cherish her, etc.) If a man has that kind of attitude towards his wife, there should be little problem with issues of authority and submission.

The establishment of the New Covenant represents a major breakthrough in the status of women in communities of faith and in society in general. Women are spiritually liberated in the New Covenant because:

1. God grants total grace to women and men equally.

2. Women can have their sins forgiven just as the men.

3. They can be born again just as the men.

4. They can be filled with the Holy Spirit just as the men.

These are four dimensions of perfect equality between men and women that were not available historically until that time.

In the past, women were held in a lower position because:

1. The curse from the sin of Eve demanded that she be ruled over by the man (**Genesis 3:16**).

2. This was made worse by further sins by women throughout the centuries.

3. And worse even more by the abusive sins of men throughout the centuries.

These three elements can all be reversed by the redeeming work of the death and resurrection of the Yeshua. Again, we see women being liberated from spiritual and social oppression by the gospel.

However, there are three areas that remain in which the distinction between male and female roles remains even after the dimensions of grace and spiritual liberation mentioned above.

1. **Created Order** - The first dimension of a continuing pattern of authority is the order of creation. Man was created first and the woman was created second as a helpmeet to him (**Genesis 2:18, I Timothy 2:13**).

2. **Child Care** - The second area has to do with granting enough time and energy for children and grandchildren. While men and women share the responsibility equally for raising the children, there is a dimension of child care that is greater with women than men. This care demands much attention to ensure the moral and spiritual development of the children.

3. **Christ and the Church** - The third area has to do with the image of man and woman representing Christ and the Church (**Ephesians 5:21-33**). There should be a sweet cooperative submission in the marriage that reflects our perfect relationship with Yeshua Himself.

Let us believe together to release the women in our midst to all their spiritual gifts and callings, and at the same time maintain the order given by God for men leading, while sharing the authority with women in partnership. May **"grace and truth meet together; righteousness and peace will kiss"** (**Psalm 85:10**).

(For a fuller discussion of the balance of authority and the purpose of authority to bring blessing, please see my book, *All Authority: A Handbook on Spiritual and Delegated Authority*.)

The issue of women in authority is addressed briefly here because so many ask questions on the subject. However, that is not the main purpose of this chapter. The primary point is for all of us, both men and women, to identify with Miriam's faith. Her boldness broke through barriers of unbelief. She was willing to go to any place under any conditions to find what Yeshua was doing.

She is a model of how a person's bold faith can cause breakthroughs for the Kingdom of God and pave the way for a new apostolic paradigm. Let us be like Miriam. No barrier could stop her. Let us lay hold of the purpose of God in our generation and open the door for a Kingdom breakthrough.

12

Ruth

UNITING ISRAEL
AND THE CHURCH

(BOOK OF RUTH)

Like the book of Esther, the book of Ruth tells the story of a true historical event concerning Israel that also serves as a pattern for a spiritual truth applicable to the both Israel and the Church today.

Ruth was a Gentile; not only a Gentile, but a Moabite. The Moabites were infamous for being born out of sexual immorality from the daughters of Lot, who had been influenced by the culture of Sodom and Gomorrah (**Genesis 19**). They were also known for bringing spiritual disaster upon Israel through sexual immorality in the time of Balaam at the sin of Baal Peor (**Numbers 25**).

So, she was a Gentile from a nation with a bad reputation in Israel. I think the awareness of Ruth's "Moabite" background is underestimated by most who read the book today. In Israelite eyes, the Moabite women were simply immoral.

In the story, Naomi and her family were forced into exile in Moab because of financial difficulty. There Ruth married into the family. The sons died and Naomi decided to return to Israel. (Many see this as a parable of the diaspora of the Jewish people and then their return to the land of Zion in the end.)

Naomi has two daughters-in-law, one Ruth and the other Orpah. They both seem to love her and to have come to faith in the God of Israel. (Many see this as a parable of the Christians in the countries where the Jews were scattered.) When Naomi decides to return to Israel, she is penniless and alone. She tries to convince her daughters-in-law to stay in Moab.

The first daughter-in-law is Orpah. (In Hebrew the root of the word Orpah means "back of the neck" and is sometimes used for one who "turns their back on you." In modern Israel military terminology, this root also refers to the "home-front," the areas within Israel not immediately facing the battle front; the "Oreph" (home-front) is where most of the civilian people live.)

Orpah decides to stay in Moab. But Ruth insists upon going back with Naomi. This is a brave and selfless decision. She does this for three reasons:

1. She does not want to abandon Naomi in her destitute state.

2. She has faith in the God of Israel.

3. She has a love for the Jewish people.

When Ruth insists on staying with Naomi, she makes this monumental statement: **"Your people will be my people and your God my God" – Ruth 1:16.** In Hebrew, this is a mere four words, "Amekh ami, v'elohaikh elohai" **עמך עמי ואלוהיך אלוהי**. The power of those words is historic and eternal. (The significance of these words has been simply and poignantly explained in Don Finto's masterful book *Your People Will Be My People*, which I highly recommend.)

Ruth recognized that if she believes in the God of Israel, she must also have a covenantal commitment to the people of Israel. (To some this has become symbolic of two types of Christians: the Orpah types who believe in Jesus but have no particular commitment to the Jewish people, and the Ruth types who believe in Jesus and also have a commitment to the Jewish people.)

In contrast, within modern Jewish culture, Ruth is seen as a righteous Gentile who converted to Judaism. She is seen even as the figure of someone who has converted away from Christianity to Judaism. That contrast points to some of the delicate and unfortunate divisions and misunderstandings between Jews and Christians over the centuries.

Ruth is beautiful, hardworking, loyal, submissive and righteous. The marriage of Ruth and Boaz may be seen as a biblical pattern for the covenant partnership between the Church and Israel today.

The relationship between Israel and the Nations of the world is a mystery that is woven and strewn throughout the entire Scriptures and biblical history:

- God makes a covenant with Noah with promises for all the nations of the world and confirms it with the rainbow as its sign (**Genesis 9:12-16**).

- God makes a covenant with Abraham almost a thousand years later with its sign of circumcision. The people of Abraham are to bring the Messianic seed and they are to bless the nations of the world (**Genesis 12:3**).

- Abraham's grandson Joseph is sold into slavery in Egypt and becomes ruler of the world (**Genesis 37:27-28; 41:57**).

- The nations of the world have their borders established according to the numbers of the sons of Jacob (**Deuteronomy 32:8; Acts 17:26**).

- After Israel has been established as a nation, King Solomon sets up an international Kingdom with peace among the nations, which became a model for the future

Messianic Kingdom (**I Kings 10:23-24; Micah 4:1-8; Matthew 12:42**).

- Jonah the prophet, although a loyal Israelite, is sent on a mission to bless the Gentiles of Assyria (**Jonah 1:1-2; II Kings 14:25**).

- Isaiah the prophet says that the Messiah and Israel should become the light of the nations (**Isaiah 2:3-4; 42:6; 49:6; 60:1-3**).

- Before His resurrection, Yeshua instructs His disciples to go only to the lost sheep of the House of Israel (**Matthew 10:5-6; 15:24**).

- After the resurrection, Yeshua instructs His disciples to go out from Jerusalem to ends of the earth (**Matthew 28:19; Acts 1:8**).

- Peter has a dream in which he is instructed to preach the gospel to the Gentiles (**Acts 10**).

- Paul is given the commission to take the gospel to the Gentiles and to establish the international Church (**Acts 22:21; 23:11; Galatians 2:8**).

- John has a vision of the glorified remnant of 144,000 Jewish believers in Yeshua alongside a great multitude from every nation of the world (**Revelation 7:4, 9**).

The apostle Paul particularly emphasized in his teachings that the relationship between Jew and Gentile in the Church is a great mystery. In fact, the partnership between Jew and Gentile is a major theme of all of his writings.

Paul's revelation was not primarily that the Gentiles could be saved. Peter and the early disciples already understood that point (**Acts 10-11**). What Paul understood was that after the gospel would reach the Gentiles, an international body would be formed: the "ecclesia" – The Church. This international body would include an essential partnership between Jews and Gentiles.

Paul received the revelation about the glory and fullness of the international Ecclesia and about the partnership between Jews and Gentiles within it.

Ephesians 3:4-6
How by revelation God made known to me the mystery…

My knowledge of the mystery of Christ…

which was not made known in generations past to men, but is now being revealed to His holy apostles and prophets through the Spirit, that the Gentiles are to be partners of the inheritance, partners in the body and partners in the promise in Messiah Yeshua by the gospel.

One of the central mysteries of the Ecclesia is that it demonstrates a partnership between Jew and Gentile. This is not a side issue.

The partnership between Jew and Gentile is an essential and central aspect of what the Church is.

The words "mystery" and "partnership" are both used three times in this short passage in Ephesians chapter 3. The mystery is in the partnership. There is a partnership of the inheritance, a partnership of the body and a partnership of the promise.

The Church is inherently a partnership between Jew and Gentile. The Church is the spiritual extension of the tribes of Israel. The Church is an international expression of the nation of Israel. The New Covenant joins the Gentiles together with Israel just as a marriage joins the family of the husband together with the family of the wife.

This aspect of the Church is essential to its very nature. When the mystery of this partnership is fulfilled, then the full purposes and wisdom of God will be revealed:

Ephesians 3:9-10
To make all see what is the fellowship of the mystery... to the intent that now through the Church the manifold wisdom of God will be made known to the powers and principalities in the heavens.

It is the partnership between Jew and Gentile in the Church-Ecclesia that reveals the manifold wisdom of God. A similar revelation is described in **Romans 11** in Paul's parable about the Gentiles being grafted into the Olive Tree of Faith with Israel.

Romans 11 and **Ephesians 3** are parallel but opposite passages. Both speak of the mystery of God being revealed. Both speak of Israel and the Church. **Romans 11** speaks of the attitude of the Church toward Israel. **Ephesians 3** speaks of the attitude of Israel toward the Church. The fullness of the Church releases the salvation of Israel; and the fullness of Israel releases the destiny of the Church. In other words, there is an interdependent cause and effect. There are two parallel processes taking place:

Ephesians 3: Israel's understanding the Church – causes – Fullness of the Church.

Romans 11: The Church's understanding Israel – causes – Fullness of Israel.

Romans 11:25-26 – I do not want you to be ignorant of this mystery, lest you be wise in your own opinion, that blindness in part has happened to Israel until the fullness of the Gentiles has come in.

And so all Israel will be saved...

When the Church comes to a full understanding about Israel, Israel comes to salvation. The words **"and so"** are important. Israel does not come to its own salvation. At the fullness of the Church, the Church receives revelation about Israel. With that revelation, the Church prays for Israel. As the Church prays for Israel, revival is released, and all Israel is saved.

The revelation of the partnership between Israel and the Church brings about the manifest wisdom of God through the Church (**Ephesians 3:10**) as well as the salvation of all Israel (**Romans 11:26**). These great mysteries described by Paul the apostle were lived out and embodied by Ruth over a thousand years before Paul was born.

This Moabite woman of humility, integrity, service and loyalty changed history. Her path was not easy. She had to give up everything she had. She left everything to go to the land of Israel just as Abraham had done. She suffered ridicule and rejection for being a non-Jew. She had to do menial, slave-labor type work in the field. She had to fend off the advances of young men on the one hand and use her feminine wiles on the other hand to attract Boaz.

(This strikes me as an ironic fulfillment of the destiny of the Moabite women. As their feminine wiles brought disaster on Israel at Baal Peor in **Numbers 25**, so did Ruth use her Moabite feminine wiles to draw Boaz into his Kingdom destiny.)

Today, this "Ruth" calling is accomplished in prayer. The Lord is raising up a mighty company of modern-day "Ruths," both men and women, to bring about the unity between Israel and the Church. They too will have to suffer the ridicule and rejection that Ruth did. Through the humility and humiliation of these modern day "Ruths," the mysteries that Paul prayed for will be revealed. Their suffering embodies both the destiny of the Church and the salvation of Israel.

The marriage of Ruth and Boaz gave birth to Obed, who was the father of Jesse, who was the father of David (**Ruth 4:17**). The marriage between Boaz and Ruth as Jew and Gentile was a necessary foundation for the future of the Kingdom of God. In our spiritual perspective, Israel-loving Christians are like Ruth, and Church-loving Jews are like Boaz. They are the link pins between Israel and the Church.

As the marriage between Ruth and Boaz brought about the birth of King David, so this company of spiritual "Ruths" will pave the way for the return of Yeshua to rule and reign on David's throne. Are you called to be part of that company?

Many Christians today are receiving this revelation and making this covenantal commitment. I have seen it happen during large assemblies in Europe, in South America, and in Asia. At the 2014 Homecoming 822 conference in Jerusalem (in response to the repentance of the Messianic leaders as described in a previous chapter), David Demian led three thousand Chinese, Arab and international Christians to proclaim out loud as a covenant vow, "Your people will be my people."

I used to think that there were two options for Christians. That the vast majority were called to be like Orpah – to believe in Yeshua but have no real commitment to Israel, while only a small percentage were to have a special, rare and unusual "Ruth-like" calling to be joined into Israel. But a shift is taking place that is revealing something else.

The covenantal connection of Christians worldwide to Israel is supposed to be the "normative" option. It should be the majority. Only those who miss the monumental revelations about Israel and the Church will take the Orpah option. (I do not mean here that all Christians are called at this time to move to Israel or to marry Jewish people. That option is still only for a small minority. I am referring to the sense of the Church worldwide accepting its covenant connection with the Jewish people and identifying with Israel as a nation.)

If there is to be a "Ruth" company, there must also be an equivalent "Boaz" company on the other side. These are Jewish people who have a heart to love the Church, the international Ecclesia. I desire to be one of those. I believe it is time for the Messianic Jewish community to embrace the international Body of Christ as our spiritual brothers and sisters.

If Yeshua loved the ecclesia as His own body, as His own bride, as His own people, then so should I. If the Church is beautiful to Him, then she must be beautiful to me as well. Can we Jews say to Gentile Christians all over the world, "Your people will be my people and your God my God?"

The Jews are my people and Israel is my nation. However, if I understand this aspect of the gospel correctly, then through Messiah Yeshua I am also betrothed to this international ecclesia as my own fiancée in a way. If the Church is Yeshua's bride, then I am part of the marriage as well. We are one together. We are a spiritual family. They have already believed in the God of Israel. We have the same spiritual "Father."

At the time of this writing, my two older sons have been married to two most wonderful and beautiful young ladies. When they were married, their wives became part of our family. In addition, we became an extended family with the families of the wives. The marriage covenant of our sons brought us into a covenantal-type relationship with the families of their wives. In the same way, as I am a believer in Yeshua, I have a covenantal-type relationship with the extended family of the international Church.

Afterword

THE MASTER PLAN FOR THE ONE NEW MAN

BY JANE HANSEN HOYT

As Asher so beautifully expresses in the last chapter of his book, using the story of Ruth, we understand the partnership between Jew and Gentile, Israel and the Church, as the essence of the Kingdom of God. From the very beginning, God had a plan for male and female, Jew and Gentile, and the parallels between them are striking.

A God of Purpose

To begin, we know that before God said, *Let there be light*; before He said, *Let there be a firmament*; before God spoke the world into being, He had a plan. Just one plan - Plan A. No Plan B. No contingency plans. Just one plan that He would ensure would come to pass.

From Genesis to Revelation, it is clear that God is a God of eternal purpose. Job stated: **I know that You can do everything, and that *no purpose of Yours* can be withheld from You (Job 42:2**, emphasis mine).

In **Isaiah 46:9-10**, God says:

Remember the former things of old, for I am God, and there is no other, I am God, and there is none like Me, declaring the end from the beginning, and from ancient times things that are not yet done, saying, "My counsel shall stand, and I will do all My pleasure."

These words tell us that we can expect every prophetic purpose God has spoken since the beginning of time to be restored and fulfilled.

One of those prophetic purposes is stated in **Ephesians 2:15** to create *One New Man* - Jew and Gentile - reconciled to each other and reconciled to God through the death and resurrection of Yeshua the Messiah.

For he himself is our peace, who has made the two one and has destroyed the barrier, the dividing wall of hostility, by abolishing in his flesh the law with its commandments and regulations. His purpose was to create in himself one new man out of the two, thus making peace, and in this one body

**to reconcile both of them to God through the cross, by which
he put to death their hostility. He came and preached peace to
you who were far away and peace to those who were near. For
through him we both have access to the Father by one Spirit.
(Eph 2:14-18 NIV)**

Key Words

There are key words for us in this passage. The first is the
word *peace*: Yeshua Himself is our peace and has broken down
the wall of hostility, or *the middle wall of separation* (NKJV),
between Jew and Gentile. That which separated, the Law and its
commandment, was abolished *in his flesh*.

The separation in the natural realm between Jew and Gentile,
and in the spiritual realm, between men and God, was typified
by the wall in the Temple dividing the court of the Gentiles from
that of the Jews, and the veil in the Temple which separated all
but the High Priest from the Holy of Holies. Yeshua, in his flesh,
broke down that wall by fulfilling the Law and its requirements
for peace with God and with each other.

One New Man is another key for us in this passage. When Yeshua
died on the cross and rose again, He made the way for all the
contention between Jew and Gentile to be removed so that a new
spiritual body made up of both could be established - One New
Man. He not only reconciles the two to each other, but actually
incorporates both into one new body of believers. Faith in Yeshua
and His completed work on the cross unites us and gives us a
joined identity as the body of Messiah.

Reconcile is the third key word in this passage. Reconciliation sets God's people apart in a way that nothing else can. Reconciliation is a foundational doctrine of the Gospel. In the New Testament, the concept of reconciliation contains the idea "to change thoroughly" (Greek *katallasso*), "to change thoroughly from one position to another" (*apokatallatto*). Reconciliation, therefore, means that someone or something is completely altered and adjusted to a specific standard. By the death and resurrection of Messiah, the world is changed in its relationship to God. By the death and resurrection of Messiah, Jew and Gentile are changed in their relationship to each other.

God's prophetic purpose revolves around unity. The goal of Plan A is bringing together, **until we all reach unity in the faith and in the knowledge of the Son of God and become mature, attaining to the whole measure of the fullness of Messiah (Eph. 4:13 NIV).** In His prayer for His disciples, Yeshua revealed the reason unity is so important: **May they be brought to complete unity to let the world know that You sent Me and have loved them even as You have loved me (John 17:23 NIV).**

In Yeshua, we have peace instead of hostility, unity instead of separation, access to the Father and reconciliation with God and other people. In that reconciliation, *we know that we are loved by God*. The world, witnessing that love, has the opportunity to see the loving hand of God extended to them.

It Is Not Good...

The obvious challenge to unity is separation. Paul spoke in **Ephesians 2** specifically about separation between Jew and Gentile, but in **Galatians**, he added to the list:

For you are all sons of God through faith in Messiah Yeshua. For as many of you as were baptized into Messiah have put on Messiah. There is neither Jew nor Greek, there is neither slave nor free, there is neither male nor female; for you are all one in Messiah Yeshua. And if you are Messiah's, then you are Abraham's seed, and heirs according to the promise (Galatians 3:26-29).

As the *One New Man* - the body of Messiah there will be no separation between Jew and Gentile, slave or free, male or female. This does not mean that faith in Messiah makes everyone the same. Jews do not stop being Jews when they become followers of Messiah. Gentiles do not stop being Gentiles. Faith in Messiah, however, eliminates the separateness. Jew and Gentile stand together in Messiah as equals joined by a common purpose and a common source of life.

Galatians tells us that the idea of unity, of breaking down the wall of separation, is not exclusively a matter of bringing together Jew and Gentile. The problem of separation existed long before there was a distinction between Jew and Gentile. God identified separation as "not good" even before sin entered the world.

Genesis 1:31 tells us that when God finished the work of creation, He **saw everything that He had made, and *indeed it was very good*** (emphasis mine). He then created Adam (see Gen. 2:7) and gave him this instruction: **Of every tree of the garden you may freely eat; but of the tree of the knowledge of good and evil you shall not eat, for in the day that you eat of it, you shall surely die (Gen. 2:16-17).** In the next verse, God said, *It is not good* **that the man should be alone; I will make him an help meet suitable for him (Gen. 2:18, KJV).**

Everything up to this point was "very good." But now, something was "not good."

What exactly was not good and why? Adam being alone seems to be the key thought in what God expresses here as "not good." The Hebrew word translated alone literally means *separation.* Man was not merely lonely; his "separation" was of a spiritual nature. To me, it speaks of an inner aloneness. George Berry's <u>The Interlinear Literal Translation of the Hebrew Old Testament</u> translates Genesis 2:18 this way: *Not good is being the man to his separation.*

Even before the fall, separation was identified as a hindrance to man's purpose and God's plan. Adam had not yet been joined to God in His "divine life." For Adam to fulfill the purpose of God, he would have to choose to receive divine life. *The purpose of God is for Adam to choose the fruit of the tree of life with his own volition so that he might be related to God in divine life* (Watchman Nee). So his separation was spiritual. His aloneness was "not good."

There was a problem in paradise and God purposed to resolve it. Help was on the way help suitable for the need. The appearance of the woman created the most fundamental relationship known to mankind. God also instituted the same principles for unity that work in every other relationship. By examining God's plan for male/female interaction, we will see principles of God's Master Plan that illustrate how Jew and Gentile can live in unity as One New Man. A remarkable number of parallels apply.

Multiplication by Division

When God created Adam, He made him in the full image of Himself. But when God took the woman from the side of the man, what happened to that image of God? Was it added to? Was it subtracted from? It was neither. It was divided.

God solved the problem of Adam's separateness by dividing. And now, for the image of God to be seen and felt and known and heard and observed in the earth, it must come through both the man and the woman. As they stood together in the garden, this was a picture of Israel and the Church to come. Male and female together comprised the structure through which God chose to begin to reveal Himself and make Himself known in the earth. It could never come through men alone; it could never come through women alone. It has to be expressed through the two of them together.

From the beginning of the world, God has shown us what dominion would look like: it was male and female. Adam and Eve became "one flesh," yet maintained their individual identities. God took from Adam's side a bride, the foreshadowing of another bride that was yet to come. Eve was like Adam in terms of her humanity, but radically different from him in other ways.

God had fashioned her and made her what she needed to be to walk with Adam as his other self - his counterpart. She was God's idea, and together they were God's design for the fulfillment of His plan of subduing the earth and taking dominion over it. God called her a help that was "meet," meaning "suitable" and adequate for him, one who could come alongside him and walk with him in a deeply purposeful way.

The first parallel, then, that we should note is that being One New Man does not mean that Jew and Gentile must become something that they are not. The differences between us were part of God's design, so that each could bring something of value to the relationship. God chose Israel as His people in order to bring reconciliation to the entire world. Gentiles have unique characteristics purposefully intended to provide suitable or adequate help: They are to help each other.

Divine Help, Human Help

What does "help" look like? Again, by looking at God's design for the first man and woman, we see a picture of God's Master Plan. The Hebrew word for help, *ezer*, means "to surround, to protect, to aid, succor." Webster's definition of *succor* is "help, to run under, to give aid or assistance in time of distress." *Help* or *ezer* is an extremely strong word, used 21 times in Scripture. Sixteen times it refers to divine help (God Himself) and five times to human help, but always in the context of help in time of trouble or help against one's enemies. The use of the word itself reveals God's intent in sending Adam a help. God had fashioned the woman in such a unique way that she would be used to surround and protect Adam.

God did not send Adam a fishing buddy or a coach. He sent him a woman because then, as now, it is the woman who is uniquely crafted by God to touch his heart, to engage his heart and to help him open his heart to her and to God.

Eve represents both human and divine help in that she was fashioned and sent from the hand of God. The emphasis was on the divine quality of the help she brought to Adam. In **Psalm 121:1-2**, the word "help" reflects this definition: **I will lift up my eyes to the hills from whence comes my help? My help comes from the LORD, Who made heaven and earth.**

She is not the man's savior, but she can be used to open and engage his heart in relationship at a deeper level, hence, bringing him out of his aloneness. She will also complete him in their role as dominion takers - those who move in divine displacement of God's enemy, Satan. She was fashioned by the Father's hand and sent from His heart into a situation that needed help.

What would happen if Gentiles, instead of seeing themselves as replacements for Israel, began to think in terms of being a suitable help, grafted into Israel to *surround, to protect, to aid, to succor* God's chosen people? Could that be what Paul had in mind when he told the Romans that Israel had not stumbled beyond recovery (see **Rom. 11:11**)?

I am talking to you Gentiles. Inasmuch as I am the apostle **to the Gentiles, I make much of my ministry in the hope that I may somehow arouse my own people to envy and save some of them (Romans 11:13-14 NIV).**

Paul, the Jew, was an apostle to the Gentiles, bringing the good news of the Jewish Messiah to them, looking to them for help in the reconciliation of Israel to God. Paul understood the importance of each part of the body of Messiah bringing its own unique gift into the relationship for the whole to be healthy.

Side by Side

Equality and Unity are inherent in the biblical description of the creation of woman:

God caused a deep sleep to fall on Adam, and he slept, and He took one of his ribs, and closed up the flesh in its place. Then the rib which the LORD God had taken from man He made into a woman, and He brought her to the man (Genesis 2:21-22).

Eve was not fashioned from a place under Adam's foot; nor was she taken from his shoulder, his elbow, his hip, or some other part of his body. She was drawn from his side because she was created to walk side by side with him in a meaningful, powerful, authoritative way; the two of them together would then be fruitful, be blessed and walk in dominion on the earth.

Eve's creation from the side of Adam teaches us that she was part of him, an extension of himself. When she was created, part of him was removed and returned to him in a very different package. The woman was not formed of new elements; she was not taken from the dust, hence, separate or independent from the man in that sense. She was part of who he was. He understood this, and

160

delighted in it, saying, **This is now bone of my bones and flesh of my flesh, she shall be called Woman, because she was taken out of Man (Gen. 2:23).**

Adam identified with Eve, recognizing the vital part she played in fulfilling his own purpose. Different as they were in so many ways, they were one in purpose. So closely were they joined that Adam could easily envision them as one flesh, as one person.

Bone of my bones and flesh of my flesh is an apt illustration of God's idea of unity. Paul's description of the One New Man expresses the same idea in slightly different words, but still with the idea of a unified body:

This mystery is that through the gospel the Gentiles are heirs together with Israel, members together of one body, and sharers together in the promise in Messiah Yeshua (Ephesians 3:6 NIV).

The Church was Jewish at its inception. The first Gentile believers did not start a separate, Gentile Church. They joined in fellowship with Jewish brothers and sisters. They were one. They supported each other, prayed for each other, encouraged one another and helped one another just as they would in a healthy marriage.

As the Gospel spread, the number of Gentiles in the Church grew proportionately until the Church was more Gentile than Jewish. In a very real sense, the Gentile church was created from the "side" of the Jewish church. And the relationship between the two grew out of that division in much the same way. Just as

Adam and Eve stood side by side, jointly fulfilling God's purpose, each contributing unique strength and vitality to the process, so Jew and Gentile are called to stand side by side.

His intent was that now, through the church, the manifold wisdom of God should be made known to the rulers and authorities in the heavenly realms, according to his eternal purpose which he accomplished in Christ Jesus our Lord (Ephesians 3:10-11 NIV).

Understanding God's Original Design

The One New Man was created to declare God's wisdom. What exactly is God's original design? The Master Plan is for unity. Growth and dominion are ambitious goals that no one can accomplish alone. It takes the joint effort of the whole body of Messiah, Jew and Gentile, male and female. Unity is essential and always has been. He clearly revealed His plan and intention in Adam and Eve. It is worth looking at it because it is still God's intention for His people. It is further exemplified in His intention for the One New Man.

In **Genesis 1:27-28**, we can see that male and female were originally designed and created to express God's image on earth. They were to be fruitful, multiply, subdue the earth and take dominion over it. Through them God intended to manifest Himself - His nature, His character and His authority, displaying His indisputable power over the works of darkness, thus subduing His archenemy, Satan.

What Does This Mean?

The idea of *being fruitful and multiplying* is often applied strictly to the realm of marriage and family; while it does apply, it goes far beyond physical reproduction. *To multiply* means "to be in authority, to enlarge; to increase." This is about the increase and multiplication of God's life and authority in us, individually and corporately - and it is about the will of heaven being brought forth on earth.

God *blessed them*, and in the original sense of the word *bless*, He was enabling them to walk in victory over their enemies, subduing and taking dominion over every foe that would arise against God's revealed plan. This is the thread that runs throughout the Word of God. It was set in place from the beginning.

Look at the words *subdue* and *dominion*. The word subdue means: *to conquer, tread down, force, keep under, and bring into subjection.* The word dominion means: *to prevail against, to take or to rule over.*

Clearly, mankind was made to walk in authority. This was the word given to God's first "image bearers," the man and woman together. Satan had already fallen like lightning from heaven (see **Luke 10:18**). This was the enemy they were instructed to guard against, to subdue. Satan was the one who had boldly declared that he intended to *exalt [his] throne above the stars of God* and *be like the Most High* (**Isa. 14:13-14**). God had already declared war on His enemy. Satan's rebellion was to be dealt with. God would use mere humans to subdue the one who had formerly officiated in the heavenly realms. In response, Satan attempted to put his enemies at enmity with each other - male against female, Gentile against Jew.

An Attempt to Undermine God's Plan

I do not think it was happenstance that the enemy approached the woman first in the garden. He who led the rebellion in heaven now seeks to continue it on earth. He was after the plan of God.

Satan was present when God said that man's aloneness was not good. He knew that God had fashioned a "help" suitable for man - a help who would walk with him and, most importantly, be the expression of dominion in the earth with him that God had intended. He knew that she had a highly significant place in man's life and in God's plan.

In approaching the woman first in the garden, perhaps Satan knew that in order to disrupt the plan of God, his best strategy would be to attack the help God sent. Satan ultimately purposed to silence the woman, to render her useless and powerless in the man's life, but further, to so weaken her in God's ultimate plan that the whole plan would be ineffectual.

One only has to look at the breakdown of the family structure and society, the growing rejection of long-accepted morals and standards, and the war against the definition of marriage as a union between a man and a woman to realize that we are in a spiritual war beyond anything the Church could have imagined in past times. The liberal press, the gay agenda and the rise of Islam in the world are not just threats to Christianity but also strikes against God Himself. They represent an anti-Messiah spirit that is coming against the very plan of God, the very structure He set in place from the beginning - that of the union, the strength, the dominion God intended for the man and woman.

It is also not coincidental that anti-Semitism has been so prevalent throughout history. Satan has attempted to eliminate the very existence of Jews for the same reason he has attacked women. He seeks to disrupt the plan of God. The prophets of Israel declared over and over that the redeemer of mankind, the one who would bring reconciliation to the world, would not only come through a woman, He would come specifically through a Jewish woman.

Satan's efforts to destroy Israel have been unsuccessful in spite of centuries of hatred and overt genocide. Unable to carry out that plan, he has sought to keep Jews and Gentiles separated. Just as he saw the importance of Eve to God's purpose for Adam, he recognized that Jews and Gentiles standing together in unity to fulfill God's plan would utterly destroy him.

The Church must see what is taking place and begin to move into a greater place of authority, but this cannot happen without the Church first seeing the strength of the place of those whom Satan seeks to separate. This includes the woman and the help she was designed to be not only in a marriage union, but also as a voice within the Church, the family and society. It also includes the diversity represented by both Jew and Gentile. It is the hour for the Church to awaken and arise to its fullest capacity and take dominion.

Exposed!

I said earlier that the principles involved in this issue of unity were the same, regardless of the nature of the wall of separation. Satan's opposition to the unity between Jew and Gentile stem from the same motivation and creates many of the same problems for mankind. Note some of the similarities.

God's plan for the original union of man and woman was for them to have dominion over the earth and to "multiply," that is, to enlarge and increase. God blessed them for the purpose of fulfilling His plan.

In much the same way, Israel was chosen to be the first fruits of humanity in order that they might become a blessing to the Gentiles. Unity between the two would fully establish God's dominion, His kingdom, on the earth.

It was not good for man to be alone, or specifically, to be separated. Neither was it good for Israel to be alone and separated. As Eve was a helper for Adam, designed to *surround, to protect, to aid, to succor,* God intended that Gentile believers should do the same for Israel, assisting and partnering in the mission of establishing the Kingdom of God. Israel was designed to give birth to and to nurture the Messianic hope of the world. Just as Adam and Eve were created to fulfill specific roles in God's Master Plan for the family, so Jew and Gentile were designed to play key parts in His plan for the earth and for mankind.

Just as it was not happenstance that Satan attacked Eve first, his desire to eliminate Jews from the earth is intentional. **Genesis 3** reveals the reason for the ongoing abuse and suppression of women throughout history and to this day. Following the tragic events of the Fall, God came in the cool of the evening, and in response to God's questions, Eve responded, **The serpent *deceived* me, and I ate (Gen. 3:13).** It was the woman who first exposed the enemy for who he really is - the deceiver. She had exposed God's enemy and God spoke into that, in essence saying, *Now forever and ever, Satan, down through the centuries she will be used again and again to expose you and to call you who you really are!*

Satan's particular hatred of women comes from his understanding that the Seed of woman would crush him (**Genesis 3:15**). Satan's hatred of Israel is based on the same type of understanding. He knew that the Messiah, the Savior of the world, would come through the Jews. Just as he has attacked women throughout history, attempting to silence and incapacitate them, he has sought the marginalization and the destruction of Israel, hoping to disrupt God's ultimate Master Plan. That plan is a covenant that God made with Israel, and God will never break His covenant.

Who's Whose Enemy?

We often refer to Satan as our enemy, but in a very real way the exact opposite is true. We are his enemy! He has known this truth from the beginning, for God stated it directly to him in relation to the woman.

Eve was the first to be ensnared by Satan and the first to expose his true nature. She was also the subject of the first promise of deliverance:

When the fullness of the time was come, God sent forth his Son, made of a woman, made under the law, to redeem them that were under the law, that we might receive the adoption as sons (Galatians 4:4-5 KJV).

Through the Seed of the woman, *[sin and] death [would be] swallowed up in victory* (**1 Cor. 15:54**). Through the Seed of the woman, God would *[disarm] principalities and powers, [making] a public spectacle of them, triumphing over them in it* (**Col. 2:15**). Heaven and earth's greatest victory would be realized out of the greatest point of defeat.

Note in this verse that the fullness of time has also revealed the close connection between man and woman, and Jew and Gentile. God sent forth His Son as a man, born of woman, under the Torah, as a Jew, to redeem the Jews and to make possible the adoption as sons of Gentiles.

The unity of Jew and Gentile is an absolutely essential element in God's plan. The One New Man transcends the differences between the two, joining their individual strengths for establishing the Kingdom of God. Walking together in the power and love of God, nothing can stop them from fulfilling God's purpose.

Separation results in loss. When the Jewish person becomes so proud of his heritage as God's chosen that he holds the Gentile at a distance, he will never be able to benefit from the support, encouragement, and strength Gentile believers have to offer. When a Gentile believer thinks of himself as Israel's replacement, he will never be able to surround, protect, aid, and succor Israel in establishing God's dominion. Instead they will remain separate, alone. And alone is not good.

To achieve the unity God wants, it is equally essential that we learn to live in unity at the most foundational level of human existence. It will be difficult, if not impossible, for Jew and Gentile to learn mutual respect and cooperation if they do not fully practice respect and cooperation at the basic level of gender relations. This is part of the reason for the passion I feel about the position of women in the Church and in society.

That They May Be One

Yeshua prayed: ...**that they all may be one, as You, Father are in Me, and I in You; that they also may be one in Us, that the world may believe that You sent Me (John 17:21).**

As we move toward the culmination of the age, just as God used a man and a woman to usher in His first coming, so God will bring the genders together, as well as Jew and Gentile, as one new humanity to prepare the way for His Second Coming. We, as His body, are being reconciled, one to another: male and female, and Jew and Gentile, so that *the world may believe;* so that the body of Messiah may manifest His glory; so that we may walk in His authority, subduing and taking dominion in the earth and fulfilling the mandate God has given us as His people. The reconciled, reunified body of Messiah is truly the "One New Man."

Asher and Betty Intrater serve on the senior leadership teams at Ahavat Yeshua Congregation in Jerusalem, Tiferet Yeshua Congregation in Tel Aviv, Revive Israel Ministries, and Tikkun International. Asher is also one of the founding board members of the Messianic Jewish Alliance of Israel. He holds degrees from Harvard University, Baltimore Hebrew College and Messiah Biblical Institute. Asher has authored *All Authority, Covenant Relationships, The Apple of His Eye, The Five Streams, From Iraq to Armageddon, What does the Bible Really Say about the Land?, Who Ate Lunch with Abraham?* and *Israel, the Church and the Last Days* (co-authored with Dan Juster). Revive Israel's weekly e-mail teaching and prayer update is currently being translated into 14 different languages.

For more information, and to receive ministry updates, please visit

WWW.REVIVEISRAEL.ORG